IMPACTS BEYOND THE BOUNDS

Explosive Success For Atypical People

BILL DEFRIES

ISBN: 9781790435319

Imprint: Independently published

Printed in the United States of America

This is a work of creative nonfiction. Events are portrayed to the best of Bill DeFries' memory. All the stories in this book are true to the author's recollection although some names and identifying details have been changed to protect the privacy of the individuals involved.

DEDICATION

To struggling students, young professionals fresh out of school, military Veterans, and anyone looking to improve their situation and pursue their dreams, desires, and big ideas.
Here are my grenades.

CONTENTS

FOREWORD

Everyone knows it—you never really know who your friends are. It's so much easier to conceal than reveal a motive, a truth, or an agenda. You might as well get hip to the notion we are generally only watching appearances of attorneys and ambassadors acting as agents for the people in front of us. Only time and a change of circumstances will show you who was really there all along. On the upside, sometimes this statement is true only because who you know is so young, their lives have not unfolded sufficiently to make a description accurate.

The reader will be glad to know this about Bill DeFries. A lot had to happen, and he had to do a lot of things before he became who he is.

I knew him before all that, but anyone who knew him in the Marine Corps was always carrying a persistent suspicion that he'd probably distinguish himself.

I fondly recall we were arrested together, along with our other roommate, Renny Wetzel, in the early spring of 1982 in Myrtle Beach. The mayor of Myrtle Beach was involved in the incident, and it was the mayor who instructed the policeman to have us arrested on an issue so minor the cop himself didn't even want to log the infraction. We sat there, the three of us, in the back of the police car, and on the way to the station, nervous and morose. I saw Bill and Renny put their heads together and whisper, evidently coming up with something, naturally enough, leaving me out of it, and then Bill spoke up and said to the cop taking us in, "Sir, I understand you have to follow orders, but you don't know this: Two of us here are Military Policemen. We are cops, like you are, and getting arrested is going to have an impact on our service records way out of proportion to the reason you've got us here. You see what I mean?"

The cop stopped the car, turned around to launch some qualifying questions to verify that my roommates were indeed cops, and he let us go, wishing us well and hoping we could still have a good time in Myrtle Beach. (We did.)

In that anecdote the reader can, after reading this book, come back for review and find most of the principles of Bill's success very much in play long before he had a way to encode them so helpfully. That has all to do with raising your hand, framing a failure, doing the next thing, patching the biggest holes, wearing your badges, planning when others wing it, or when others, like me, are too drunk to know what's going on, persisting together, and transforming by leadership. That situation was transformed.

Many times in the course of this book, a situation of considerable adversity is transformed into something else entirely, and since adversity cannot be avoided on this tricky belligerent planet, knowing how to bring that about is very important. The crisp way Bill renders his recipe is so handy, he makes it easy to learn and hard to forget; it's an advantage easily gained at exactly the point where an advantage is going to be decisive. The reader encounters many times here a predicament which will either lead to a predictably mournful outcome, or by following the principles Bill DeFries outlines here, an unexpected flourishing new result. Anyone who values their own struggle will prefer the latter, or else they are just too stupid to read.

We lived for a time in that year at 306 North Shore Drive, Surf City, North Carolina. We were the boys of the town, and the storekeeper always had several cases of Black Label beer up front for us. We wanted to be bohemians, but we were Marines, so we could not be bohemians. I wonder if we could be called the Fighting Bohemians of Surf City? That would be nice. Bill must be forgetting that I smoked in the house, because I always did, and so did everyone, and I still do. The girls, Pinero and Bergeron, sure did, and I don't remember that Bill was scolding them. No matter.

One of the Fighting Bohemians of Surf City, with hair pomaded and a carefully gathered silk robe he had picked up in Japan, came out of his room to greet the girls wearing, of all things, ascot. Somehow he had the sense of couth and the daring to don ascot for the evening, and he gave us that kind of a gunfighter's grin that held any sneering in contempt. Renny Wetzel made a thing out of it by saying, "There he is: the number one most glamorous male model throughout the universe and across all time, Bill DeFries. Everybody bow, everybody get in line for his autograph!" The trouble was that the ascot was so appropriate on him no clever remarks could detract from it, so he kept it on.

When you're in the Marine Corps, you cannot be distinguished any more than one blade of grass can be distinguished from another blade of grass in a field of grass, but by his own sense of pluck, Bill was distinguished, and furthermore, he could see things that other people didn't, and he was looking for things that others were not in search of.

From that time, and this was before half my mind was blown away in combat overseas, I remember reading, in one of those books Bill remembers I was reading, something that Philip Levine wrote:

And they salute as one and stand at peace.
Keeping an arm's distance from everything,
I answer them, knowing they see no face
Between my helmet and my helmet thong. [1]

DeFries could see faces where there were no faces, and he could look into confusion and stresses and see patterns, and he could look at adversity and see opportunity and better possibilities, and his book is a guide for having better vision in the world.

Reverge Anselmo

THE BATTLEFIELD OF LIFE

"Dad, I'm scared." I couldn't take my eyes off the floor. I had a huge lump in my throat, trying to control my emotions. "I don't know what I'm going to do after the...after the..."

For the first time in my life, my Dad put his arm around me. What a sight. A United States Marine sniffling and coughing through tears. An old man holding onto his grown son.

I finally found the rest of my sentence. "After the Marines. After *this*." I looked down at my uniform and government-issued sea-bag. *This is my life, and it's about to be over.*

"You know what?" Dad patted my shoulder like Mom used to. *God, I miss her. I hate cancer.*

"What?" I could feel him staring at me through those plastic frame aviators.

He gulped. "It will work out. You'll be fine."

How would you know? Another year of this, and I've got nothing to come back to. No college. No job. No connections.

"Have a seat." Dad motioned to the chairs against the wall opposite the boarding area. My flight was a few minutes away.

"What?" I dropped my bag on the floor and leaned over my knees. *Another lecture?*

"Did I ever tell you about the first Marines I ever met?"

First Marines? I knew Dad fought in the Pacific Theater in the Navy during World War II.

"No. What about them?"

"Before Guadalcanal. Before you seagoing bellhops gave the Japs hell." *A jab at the Marines. Thanks, Dad.* "There was a battalion of Marines on my ship. Most courageous sons of bitches I ever met. They knew they would be the first to hit the beaches. To take the fire. To get killed." He paused. Lost in memory. Grief, too. "The point is," he looked up at me, "every time I see you, I see those Marines. Those elite warriors who could take on anything, from bayonets to empires."

Is Dad saying...he's proud of me? That's a first.

"You're going to go back to Japan and be that tough jarhead you've become. Do your duty and serve your country like I did. Then you're going to come back. And you'll be okay." He put his hand on my knee and lowered his voice. "Believe you me, Billy boy. Believe you me."

The stewardess waved at me from behind the counter at the gate. *It's time.*

"Okay." I gave my Dad a hug. Another first. "I believe you."

He picked up my bag and walked me to the counter. "You'll be okay, son. You've got this. You'll see."

One step after the next, I headed through the door down the ramp to my seat on the plane—and to my future. A battlefield of the unknown. Then I realized something. *Dad's right.* I felt scared, hopeless, and lost. But Dad was right. Like my Marine Handbook says on the first page, "*I am an American fighting man.*" In a year, I'd be back in Chicago. I didn't know who I'd become or where I'd go or what I'd do.

"It will work out. I'll be fine," I whispered to myself.

Chicago was a city of silver skyscrapers, men in fancy suits, and noisy crowds. Between John Hancock Center to the Chicago Mercantile Exchange, I would find my place. I make something of myself and join the ranks of the successful.

Dad, I'm gonna prove you right.

🤜🤜🤜🤜

Most people who read self-help and personal success books are frustrated and dissatisfied. Since you're reading this book, I assume that includes you, too. You're not happy with your trajectory. With how things have gone or how they're shaping up. You're not happy about your career, your education, or your personal life. You're not happy with where you are, but you don't know where to go next. You're stuck in a no-man's land, and you're all out of ammo.

You're in good company. At Chicago O'Hare Airport on Christmas 1983, that was me. I wasn't happy about where I was or where I was going. In one year, my time in the United States Marines would be over. Even though I saw myself as a hopeless nobody, my Dad saw me as a brave hero. I thought he was crazy, but the truth is, I already had everything I needed.

Call me crazy, but I see the same for you, too. I wrote this book for people like me—like *you*. For people who don't live a normal life or have a "safe" career. Or any career for that matter. Maybe that opportunity passed you by, you missed it, or you never came across it in the first place.

It will work out. You'll be fine. Believe me.

The fact that you've picked up this book tells me you are ready for a change. You're besieged by uncertainty, yet you're ready for action. There *is* still time for you to be whatever you want to be. I know because I am living proof that atypical people *can* create explosive success.

After serving as a Military Policeman for four years—two in Japan and Korea—I became an automobile salesman. I set the record for most new and used cars and trucks sold in one month at one of the largest Chevrolet dealerships in America. A few years later, I earned starring roles in national fast food commercials and on the Chicago theatre scene. I joined the Screen Actors Guild-American Federation of Television and Radio Artists, a membership I've held for over twenty-five years. Later, I rose to Regional Sales Manager and CEO in the integrated security systems industry. As an entrepreneur, I now own multiple restaurants and businesses in southwest Ohio. In 2017, I was inducted into the Ohio Veterans Hall of Fame for philanthropy.

To the average person, that's one hell of a resume. But if you had known me as a young man, you would've thought success looked like a minimum wage convenience store job. What trouble-making proletariat from a lower middle class blue collar Chicago south side neighborhood makes a name for himself? I didn't have the pedigree, the education, the open doors of privilege—*but I still made it*.

The fact that you're reading this book tells me you weren't born sucking on a silver spoon either. But you can still make it, too. My Dad saw in me atypical traits —a drive to try harder than other people and pursue new opportunities even if I wasn't qualified. Ambition —he knew I had it.

I see the same qualities in you. Yes, you're afraid of the unknown like I was. You don't see a path forward through the crossfire. I didn't either. Like me, you have two choices: *You can stay here and be miserable, or you can make your own damn path forward.* It's like you're in a foxhole in battle. When you're hunkered down and can't see the enemy, you have a decision to make. Stay there, and life as you know it is over.

You're *dead*. The only thing you have left is to attack what's outside the foxhole...whatever *is* out there. And you've got grenades to blast your way out. With this book, I'm giving you "grenades"—tactical success principles—to charge out of your foxhole. Deploy these principles, and you'll move forward, be successful, and achieve your dreams, goals, and big ideas.

It doesn't matter what put you in that foxhole in the first place. Like me, you may not have credentials, but the same timeless, explosive success tactics I took to heart in 1984 are available to you today. And now I'm giving them to you. Inside my crate, you'll find ten grenades to detonate the uncertainty and win the war against mediocrity. Peek inside my crate, take a deep breath, strap a rocket on your ass, and prepare to throw all ten. You'll need them.

> *Your First Grenade: Raise Your Hand.*
> *Your Second Grenade: Frame Failure.*
> *Your Third Grenade: Do the Next Thing.*
> *Your Fourth Grenade: Patch the Biggest Holes.*
> *Your Fifth Grenade: Wear Your Badges.*
> *Your Sixth Grenade: Plan When Others Wing It.*
> *Your Seventh Grenade: Stand Up No Matter What.*
> *Your Eighth Grenade: Give, Don't Give Back.*
> *Your Ninth Grenade: Persist Together.*
> *Your Tenth Grenade: Transform by Leading.*

Use these weapons, and the tide will turn in your favor. You'll come out of life's battlefield victorious. Explosive success is *yours*. Your mission will be steeped with anticipation and fulfilment along the way. Over the coming chapters, I will prove it to you. Right now, your future is a little fuzzy. You have dreams, but no idea how to defeat the enemies and blast through the obstacles in your way. What if I told you that your dreams are your future self? But they won't become reality until you *make* them your reality. Over the next ten chapters, I will help you do just that.

Are you ready to walk through the war zone together? Because it's the only path worth walking. Promise!

RAISE YOUR HAND

"Yes is always more interesting than no."

That's what my improv coach taught me. If you haven't seen improvisational theatre before, improv is like leaping off a cliff and hoping you find a parachute before you hit bottom. Improv shows are unplanned, unscripted, and uncensored performances. All the actors have on stage is each other. If they "play off" each other well, the audience is in for a treat.

The day I showed up to my first improv class, I had no idea how hard it would be. During improv, you think, act, and speak on pure impulse. In everyday life, we don't verbalize our own thoughts this freely for fear of being criticized, judged, or (depending on the situation) *slapped*! Improv is the exact opposite. Whatever you are thinking, no matter how ridiculous, crude, or uncomfortable it may be, *say it*. Say it proudly.

In improv class, the coach encouraged us to take chances. When you're standing up on stage with someone you barely know and being instructed to tell a story, you have to work with whatever your partner gives you. If you're both the same sex and have a twenty year age difference, start breaking taboos. Blurt out something like, "Honey, we can't keep seeing each other like this," and your improv is off to a good start. Then your partner responds. You say something back. A scene unfolds. Next thing you know, the audience members are laughing their asses off. The experience replaces pulse-pounding fear with a rush of freedom.

You've found a parachute.

Of course, the real you would probably say no to most of what pops into your head. In one of my early classes, a late-teen Catholic girl turned into a drug-dealing hooker with the mouth of a sailor before our eyes (and ears). What if she had told herself no in that scene? What if she had chosen to remain comfortable? Momentum, gone. Life as we knew it on stage, dead.

"HOLD!"

Isn't this exactly what we do in real life? A new opportunity comes along. A new direction reveals itself. But it's a little bit scary. It's promising but unfamiliar. It has potential, but it feels uncomfortable. You're afraid to look like foolish, be laughed at, or be told that it's too crazy an idea. Who wants to look like an idiot on stage in front of coach and classmates?

Who wants to look like an idiot in life in front of family, friends, and coworkers?

"Nope, not interested," whispers the voice in the back of your head, and you shut down.

Improv taught me how to fight that urge. Every time you say yes instead of no—every time you raise your hand when life calls on you—you take a step forward. Life improves because *you* improve. Even if the risk may not be worth the reward, say yes. Regardless of results, yes is always more interesting than no.

Despite the stigma of car sales, I found myself in that profession for almost a decade. After I set the all-time dealership record, you would've thought I found my life's calling. But since the curtains closed on a Beverly Community Arts Center production of *Oliver!* when I was five years old, I'd been telling my parents, "I'm gonna be a professional actor someday!"

Years later, the military, a family, and a stable career seemed to cut off all routes for that opportunity to find me. When I read a quote from George Elliot one lazy Saturday, the pit of my stomach churned over itself.

It's never too late to be who you might have been.[1]

The truth hit me harder than the temper of my old drill instructor. *The greatest risk, is no—not yes.*

That weekend, I signed up for improv classes at Second City Players Workshop Theatre. During my first class, the improv coach's words—"Yes is always more interesting than no"—proved me right. Over the next few months, I left car sales, landed a small role in Robert De Niro and Kevin Costner's *The Untouchables*, and trained with Brian Stepanek. Years later, Brian starred in Disney Channel's Original Series *The Suite Life of Zack & Cody* and the *Transformers* movie. He still stars in A-list productions to this day.

When audition opportunities came my way away from stage or film, I said yes to those as well. That led to the leading role in McDonald's commercials that aired on television and radio across the nation. Even though I hadn't sung in public since kindergarten Christmas choir and neighborhood caroling, I also auditioned for a musical adaptation of Edgar Allan Poe's "The Raven." The casting director took me aside after I somehow managed to hit a note in "Daddy's Little Girl" that was two octaves higher than my normal speaking voice.

"You didn't think you could hit that high note, did you?" he asked.

My sweat-drenched palms must have given me away. I knew my buddy Brian had his eyes on the lead role, but what did I have to lose giving it my best shot? A week later, I got it.

For a year and a half, I rode the acting wave until another opportunity in a different industry came along. But that's a story for another chapter. Without saying yes, I most likely would have carried that lifelong dream with me to the grave. I could have rationalized and over-thought it—because no is practical. No is safe. No is familiar. But saying no kills an improv scene, and it kills your dreams, desires, and big ideas. No guarantees you will NEVER be what you might have been.

Whether you want to become a star or just pay off those damned student loans, taking advantage of new opportunities is your secret weapon. It just might be your *only* weapon. Think back to elementary school during a teacher's lecture. When she called on the class, what did NOBODY want to do?

Raise their hand.

There was too much risk. If you said the wrong thing, other kids might laugh at you. You might get picked on, have your lunch stolen, or worse. This fear of opportunity follows many of us into adult life. For example, I mentor college seniors at the University of Dayton. During my "Walk the Talk" discussions around business ethics, I always ask for a volunteer to take notes and present their group's sixty-second findings to the rest of the class. Rarely do I get more than one volunteer, if that. What an opportunity to develop your skills and get recognized as a leader! These students are bright and destined for career success, yet they too let fear hold them back.

We carry this aversion to hand-raising into our careers and personal lives. Most people—especially the "geniuses" among us—don't want to raise their hands and accept new opportunities. Their hesitation is your advantage. In business, there's a principle called First Mover Advantage. The first business to move on a new customer need, launch a new product, or capitalize on a new market trend is the winner who takes all. Even if other companies offer better products and faster service, the first business that raises their hand owns customers' loyalty.[2]

Be an opportunist who says yes when everyone else says no. Be the First Mover who acts *now*, before you have your shit together. Be the kid in the back of the class who raises his hand when the teacher calls. Raising your hand may be a literal action you take or an empowering state of mind. My Dad always called this "moxie."

When I was a teenager, fourteen to be exact, I got a job at the Chateau Bu-Sché, a fancy Chicago suburban banquet hall. For one dollar and ninety cents per hour, I sorted silverware. Not exactly a glamorous job, but compared to the unemployment faced by my south side neighbors, it was a vacation. After a few weeks of *scrub, wipe, clean, stack, scrub, wipe, clean, stack* in a mildew-ridden corner of the kitchen, the burly head chef named Sam threw an apron at me.

"I need help with lettuce, Billy. Wanna be the new salad guy?"

Really? A promotion?

A can-do attitude made, "Hell yes!" my automatic answer. I had no idea what my duties would include or the fact that my hourly wages would increase by ten cents, but that didn't matter. If where you could go is better than where you could stay, *go*.

That able-mindedness took me from silverware to salads to the service—the United States Marine Corps. During weapons and munitions training at Camp Pendleton in the San Onofre mountains overlooking Oceanside, California, I raised my hand. Again, this didn't necessarily include a literal raising of the hand. The Marines look down on that sort of thing when you're called to attention!

At the grenade obstacle course, standing among a few hundred recruits on aluminum bleachers, I saw an opportunity. *My* opportunity. The old, salty Marine gunnery sergeant barked at us. His voice was somewhere between a thirty-year chain smoker's cough and Emperor Palpatine's cackle in *Return of the Jedi*.

"We've got a challenge for you!" he yelled. The bare mountainside behind the bleachers reverberated with his voice. "We do this for every company, but very few men have succeeded. If you do it, you'll get yourself a soda pop. Now, here's the challenge..."

Over the next thirty seconds, I swear I saw my fellow recruits shit themselves. The task: throw a live grenade without killing anyone. The objective: land the grenade beyond the impact area about one hundred yards away.

I'm going to do this. I'm going to give it my best shot. I felt my baseball pitching arm twitch. *I'm going to prove they can count on me in battle.*

The gunnery sergeant ordered us to stand in line single file, each of us taking our turn at his challenge.

Thump.
Thump.
Thump.

The first few recruits' attempts exploded so far away we could barely hear them. Still, their grenades landed not even halfway to the far end of the impact area.

Then it was my turn. The lanky ordinance instructor motioned to join him in the launch area—a small crater with cinderblock walls all around. Black smudges on one side confirmed a rumor I'd heard in the barracks that morning. Apparently, several recruits had effed up grenade training before, killing themselves and everyone around. That wouldn't be me. I stood at parade rest with my hands folded behind my back, waiting for instructions.

"Prepare to hold." The instructor reached into his wooden crate for a grenade.

I held out an open hand, and he slipped a cold green sphere of death into my right palm. I wrapped my fingers around it and waited for the next command.

"Thumb clip. Twist. Pull pin."

I took my left index finger through the ring of the pin. I twisted and pulled the pin out. And waited.

"Prepare to throw."

I stepped back with my right foot and extended my right arm, grenade in hand, way back over my right foot, all while extending my left hand out towards the impact area horizon. I looked like I was about to throw a javelin.

"Throw!"

In a flash, the instructor was gone. No cinderblocks, mountains, or Marines. I felt the laces of a baseball in my hand. One hundred yards away, my catcher hunkered down over home plate. My crosstown rival slugger dug in his cleats after a final practice swing. I felt a warm breeze. It carried a voice from the grandstands.

"Smoke 'em, Billy! Spook 'em, Billy!"

Dad.

I raised my left leg, shifting all weight back to my right throwing arm and leg. Then, like a trebuchet, I released everything. *Everything*.

Straight down the pipe, I launched that ball directly into my catcher's mitt. Everyone heard a leathery *smack!* before the batter reached his follow through.

"Strike!" shouted the umpire.

I hit the deck in a prone position, face down, holding my family jewels.

Thump...

The diamond was a mountain again. I looked at my Dad.

"Get outta here, recruit!" yelled the instructor in my face.

The audience in the grandstands were now Marines who'd completed the obstacle course.

"Hey, look!" Someone pointed at the impact area. A small mushroom cloud of dirt, pebbles, and shrapnel rose from the impact area—no...BEYOND the impact area. A good ten yards past the far edge!

"Hey, recruit!" The gunnery sergeant called for me. "Was that you who done threw the grenade off the impact area?"

I snapped to attention so hard I pulled a muscle in my neck. "Sir, yes, sir!"

"Alright, alright..." He nodded, looking for the first time like he didn't know what to say next. "Alright then! Get outta here!"

So, I scrambled out of there to whatever was next. *I spooked 'em.*

One month to the day later, that gunnery sergeant called me into his office and handed me my favorite soda pop, a root beer. When you raise your hand, you get noticed—and it pays.

After finishing my tour in the Marines, a career in used car sales awaited me. One local connection and three job interviews later, I had a one hundred percent commission job. Long before I seriously considered the path to acting, I had bills and a mortgage to pay. At Bill Jacobs Chevrolet in Joliet, Illinois, nobody asked me to raise my hand. But I did anyway, this time trying something no one else had considered. My job: sell trucks and conversion vans. (Conversions vans are cargo vans transformed into mini-RV's with a fold-down bed, television set, lounge chairs, and a kitchenette.)

To transform a high turnover job into a six-figure career, I decided to throw a party to end all parties—

"The Bill Jacobs Midwest Conversion Van and Truck Show." Did I know what such a show needed? Absolutely not! But I did know from operating a lemonade stand with my sister as a kid that we needed an attraction. A neighbor kid who knew how to do magic tricks wouldn't work this time around. I called around and rented circus tents, sixty-foot inflatable balloons, a hovercraft, and klieg lights so bright, people could see them ten miles away. Without asking the owner's permission, I also ordered one hundred conversion vans from our regional manufacturer. I bought newspaper and TV ads for our ten-day event.

On the morning of the first day, the dealership looked like a Hollywood movie premiere. Hundreds of people who'd seen the ads—or spotlights—parked in the next door K-Mart parking lot once ours filled up. By close of business on day two, we'd sold twenty-five vans.

Over the next four weeks, I sold the remaining conversion vans, made Bill Jacobs an even wealthier man, and set the all-time dealership van sales record. Nobody asked me to put on a show like this. It wasn't in my job description. But I saw an opportunity, and I raised my hand.

Raising your hand gives you a future. Raising your hand helps you reach the next rung of the career advancement ladder. Even if your only immediate reward is a free soda pop, when you engage with new opportunities, you open the door to more. You become a person who always says yes with excitement when everyone else says no with fear.

That's exactly what happened to a carpenter in California who did his best to scrounge up enough cash to support his two toddler-age daughters. To put food on the table, he remodeled homes, built sets for theatres, and handcrafted unique props for B-list movie directors. One client liked the way he carried himself and asked if he might consider auditioning for a small budget film he'd been planning.

The carpenter raised his hand.

He won the role, portraying a smooth-talking gunslinger. The character's name was Han Solo.[3,4]

Four years before *A New Hope* became a pop culture phenomenon, a Korean family emigrated to the United States. No degrees, careers, or English language proficiency—only the clothes on their backs and the change in their pockets. The twenty-six year-old husband and wife took any jobs available to fund the American Dream for their daughters. Saving as much money as they could from the husband's jobs pumping gas, serving coffee, and cleaning toilets, they had a few thousand dollars to play with, which they put toward a retail garment store called "Fashion 21."

This Korean family raised their hands.

Today, Do Won Chang and his daughters run their business under a new name, *Forever 21,* and are worth a combined six *billion* dollars.[5]

While the Changs were busy opening up their second and third *Fashion 21* locations, two states over, reality crushed a young woman's dreams. Growing up in the segregated south, she found refuge and hope in the piano. Years of lessons landed her a college scholarship—her best chance to become a professional orchestra pianist.

But at a music festival during her sophomore year, she couldn't compete with the other pianists. Their natural abilities beat her knowledge of music theory. Two years left in her music major program but no reason to stick with it, she flipped through her college's course catalog to see what else was out there. A political science course taught by a Holocaust survivor caught her eye.

The young pianist raised her hand.

The professor, a man named Josef, capitalized on his new student's curiosity and took her under his wing. His Czech ancestry intrigued her, a black woman, so she ran to the library and got her hands on everything Eastern European she could. She learned Russian, studied communist revolutions, and memorized modern military strategies. With this firm foundation, doors of opportunity flew open for her over the coming years. On January 26th, 2005, Condoleezza Rice became the first African-American female United States Secretary of State.[6]

What do the success stories of Harrison Ford, Do Won Chang, and Condoleezza Rice have in common?

When a new opportunity presented itself, they raised their hands. I'm not promising you'll become the next Han Solo or earn a billion dollars. The point is, you wouldn't know who those people were if they hadn't raised their hands...if they'd given into fear...if they'd said no. And if I hadn't raised my hand throughout my career, you wouldn't be reading this book now. Chances are, I would still be sorting silverware back at the Chateau Bu-Sché. Professional acting? No way. A six-figure sales job? Dream on.

Someday, you can look back on your own life story and see similarities to Harrison, Do Won, Condoleezza, and entrepreneurs like me. If only you raise your hand.

So, raise your hand in your job. Raise your hand in class. Raise your hand in your neighborhood, in your city. Lots of "more qualified" people are too scared to do it—use their fear to your advantage. Get on stage and see what happens. Throw the grenade as hard as you can. Schedule an event you have no idea how to put on, then figure out how. Don't worry if you don't think you're prepared. You'll figure it out along the way. Yes, you'll make mistakes. You'll have failures. Either way, you're gaining priceless experience. It's called OJT—on the job training, and it's the best possible way to learn and succeed.

FRAME FAILURE

Be careful how you use the f-word. No, not *that* f-word. I'm talking about *failure*. Screwing up. Feeling defeated. Breaking down. Being disappointed. Blowing it.

I detest the cliché we've all heard, "Learn from your failure." What does that imply? You fail. Then you carry that failure with you. And it haunts you. For years. It's a burden you drag behind you, constantly reminding you of all those "I wish I hadn'ts" and "If only I would'ves."

In this light, failure is a terrible thing *the moment* you experience it, and it remains a terrible thing *long afterward*. Taunting you. Deriding you. Tormenting you. You're charging toward *atypical* success, remember? So, don't *learn* from you failure. Don't lug around that burden of tortured memories, wasting precious mental and emotional energy.

Instead, *frame* your failure. Put it into perspective. Use your failure as a tool to make changes or adjustments on your path. Frame your failure so that you can look closely at it, to learn from it and use it to your advantage. It's not a burden, it's a backpack of useful resources that serve you as a means to achieve success.

Although I did experience mild triumphs on stage and on camera, my acting *experience* didn't match my acting *dreams*. No major film roles came my way. I never shared a passionate on-screen kiss with a heart-throb. (But I did enjoy brief romantic moments with female co-stars in CD and ice cream commercials!) In fact, at the time of this writing, I don't even have a Wikipedia page. In show business, it doesn't get much more mediocre than that. Did I fail? That's one interpretation. But I prefer to carry a backpack of useful tools, not a burden of painful regrets..

Through improv classes, auditions, and the limited roles I did score, I learned how to speak confidently in public. Without fear, cold sweats, or second-guesses. Holding my own in front of an audience, and even feeding off their energy. From employee meetings to packed auditoriums, my public speaking skills serve me to this day.

Notice how I frame my "failure" in acting. Opportunities I would've been terrified to accept before my short acting career came naturally for me afterward. Take speaking at a Special Olympics event before an Ohio State University basketball game, for example.

Nine years after I recited my final line in a theatrical production, I opened my first restaurant—a Beef O'Brady's in Centerville, Ohio. Every single week, I met, shook hands, and chit-chatted with *four thousand* people. My acting "failure" empowered me to leave every single customer with a smile.

And when we had birthday parties to celebrate, I gathered the entire staff to put on a show for the lucky guest's special day. After lining up single file, I jogged through the restaurant singing a Public Domain version of Happy Birthday. Followed by a dozen or so clapping employees, I weaved around tables and chairs, making a spectacle of myself in front of guests. When we finally reached the birthday girl or boy, they and their families could only smile. Every employee high-fived the guest, and I personally thanked everyone in the party for celebrating at Beef's. I haven't done the math, but the value of repeat business and word-of-mouth marketing we've received is well over a million dollars. (At the time, the average Beef O'Brady's franchise annual sales were eight hundred thousand dollars. That first year, we *doubled* that—one million, seven hundred thousand dollars!)

Frame failure.

Despite the fact I never appeared on the cover of GQ as an actor, I did come away with more than a public speaking skill set. In other seasons of life, silver linings of storm clouds were harder to find. A few weeks after enlisting in the United States Marines, I found myself in front of sixteen other Marine recruits.

"DeFries, move up front to squad leader! *Hurry up!*"

At twenty years old, there I stood, wondering why I'd been chosen. Out of a squad of seventeen men, the lead Drill Instructor picked me—*me*—to be squad leader. Maybe it was my height. Or my straight-toothed smile. Or a suite of leadership abilities I didn't know I had.

Whatever the reason for picking me, I could not let my squad down. From morning bugle reveille to sundown, the squad was *my* responsibility. Every action, every behavior, every remark. To earn a promotion and higher pay after boot camp, I had to hold this leadership position for seventy-three days. For the first few weeks, everyone toed the line, speaking to superiors only when spoken to and obeying every order to the "t."

Except Bud. The squad slacker. Lazy. If he screwed up, everyone else got punished.

Day sixty-one. Laundry. The squad stood over concrete tables scrubbing our soapy uniforms against bare concrete. I caught Bud mouthing off about how sore his hands got, how it wasn't fair we had to do this. *Enough's enough.*

I laid into him in front of the entire squad. Every cuss word and mother-related insult I'd heard on Chicago's streets as a kid. I shouted so loud, the fleeing wildlife around us probably thought it was the thunder of a coming storm. Bud bit his lower lip till it bled. Tears welled at the corners of his eyes.

"You should know better!" I concluded my rant. "You're about to be a *Marine*, for God's sake."

The squad at the table next to us perked up and dropped their clothes in unison. *Busted*. Before I could attempt damage control, my temper tantrum made its way back to the Drill Instructor. No second chances, no do-overs. The DI stripped the leadership role from me and appointed another kid. My replacement got a promotion and higher salary when we graduated boot camp twelve days later.

I was *pissed*. Still, it was all my fault, and I knew it. Instead of taking responsibility for motivating Bud to behave better, I blamed him for his mistakes. Instead of encouraging him to change, I punished him when I couldn't take any more. That experience— that...*failure*—taught me to never, EVER criticize someone in front of others. Stewing alone in the barracks after my demotion, I realized that praise should be public, and discipline should be private. I'd gotten them both exactly wrong.

Years later, when I worked my way up to sales management, I remembered Bud and our "chat" on laundry day. To turn unmotivated, whiny employees a week away from the pink slip into top-performing company assets, I did what I should've done with Bud. After praising them in front of coworkers for what they *had* done well, I tactfully pulled them aside. "Let's get back to square one," I'd say. "Do good things around here, and good things will come your way." I'd verbalize my frustrations as calmly and respectfully as possible, then give the employee a chance to share their side of the story. Today, I call this approach to discipline Performance Management.

My "failure" with Bud saved dozens of disgruntled employees' jobs—and their dignity. Tales of failure can only become success stories when we reinterpret negative experiences as positive ones. Frame, don't learn. This helps you take a step back from potentially painful experiences and see the bigger picture. And many times, that picture is more beautiful—and more helpful and prosperous—than you could ever imagine.

Take the story of a nineteenth century dual between a lawyer and a politician. In the mid-1800s, a recession appeared on the Illinois horizon when the state bank went belly-up. This meant all printed currency was worth less than gum stuck to the bottom of a shoe. To cut the state's losses, the Illinois state auditor supported the decision to close the bank.

The auditor took heat for his stance, and a local lawyer and his fiancé added fuel to the fire. The couple published articles under pen names in a local newspaper. They slandered the state auditor as a cruel debtor and immoral womanizer. Furious, the auditor ordered the newspaper editor to reveal the authors' real names, and he obliged.

"Only a full retraction may prevent consequences which no one will regret more than myself," the auditor threatened.

The lawyer and his wife refused. In that day and age, reputation was everything. The greatest privilege a person could earn was a good name. To defend his from the young couple's prank, the auditor threw down the challenge.

You. Me. A duel to the death.

On September 22nd, 1842, the lawyer and auditor met on an island outside St. Louis, prepared to gut each other to death with broadswords. Fortunately, pleas from friends, family, and coworkers changed their minds. Cooler heads prevailed. The young lawyer didn't have the facts straight, and it nearly cost him his life. Failing to challenge a public figure with honor taught him to never again make an accusation without evidence.

Eighteen years later, lawyer-turned-President Abraham Lincoln calmly led a nation through civil war.[1] Even when he felt like lashing out at his seemingly incompetent generals, Lincoln kept his opinions to himself. Throughout his presidency, he wrote scathing letters of rebuke...which he never sent.[2] What good would it do to destroy soldiers' morale after a defeat on the battlefield?

Frame failure.

Even when you are not to blame for a failure, you're still in control of your reaction to it—and you *can* choose to leverage it to reach success. A century after Lincoln's attempted dual, a newly divorced mother of three pounded pavement and rang doorbells to put food on the table. She sold books, cleaning supplies, and home appliances door-to-door. She believed her southern charm, helpful attitude, and consistent results made her promotable. Her boss disagreed, choosing a guy *she* had trained for the promotion instead.

The saleswoman could've called it quits. Thrown up her hands in defeat. Cursed the evils of 1960s sexism. She didn't. Instead, this woman framed failure to receive a promotion as a sign. *Forget traditional employment. What about entrepreneurship?*

She approached a family friend who ran a small ointments business. For a few thousand dollars, the now ex-saleswoman bought her friend's ointment business. With her son's help, the proud new owner of a skincare company opened a retail storefront. She hired as many women for sales positions as possible and paid them how she wanted to be compensated at her last job. That revolutionary business model soon grew out of the retail world and touched women's lives all around the world. When she passed away in 2001, Mary Kay Ash's company Mary Kay Cosmetics sold over one *billion* dollars' worth of skincare products every year.[3]

Frame failure.

Like Abraham Lincoln, Mary Kay Ash, and everyday people like me, frame every failure in your life. They are your stepping stones to success, if only you'll let them be. Don't be so selfish to think you're the only one who's messed up. If the belief that you've failed stays locked inside your head, the only "lesson" you actually learn is that you are a failure. How useful is that? Dwelling on what could've been or what might've been pushes you off sanity's cliff, and you'll plummet into depression and heartache. One mistake becomes ten, becomes a hundred. A sour attitude at work keeps promotion out of arm's reach. A hopeless outlook on life blinds you from all the enriching opportunities that cross your path daily.

Framing my acting "failure" as public speaking *success* left me with a bright smile and a straight posture, ready to triumph at the next big thing. And it can for you, too. This is Compounding, where something's value changes exponentially over time.[4] Be grateful for your backpack, and your confidence skyrockets. But every time you rehash an experience as a "mistake," its power to hold you back grows. It's the difference between telling yourself, "I will use this experience to my advantage," and "I will let this experience *use me* to my *dis*advantage."

Which will it be?

DO THE NEXT THING

I feel like a Millennial. People tell Millennials to pick one career path and stick with it. To mortgage the future and pile up student loan debt. To sacrifice multiple potential careers for *one* that may or may not be the best fit. High school guidance counselors. College and career fairs. Friends and family. They all mean well.

Back in the 1990s, people starting their careers changed jobs only twice in their first decade in the workforce. Today, it's double. Millennials change jobs *four* times in the ten years after college.

"Millennials are entitled and irresponsible," the experts say. "Employers shouldn't trust them!"

Bullshit. The powers-that-be who tell you to pick one career path are as wrong as they are impractical. Life changes. Technology evolves. Industries rise and fall. Unlike most Baby Boomers, I've never wanted to stay at the same company for forty years, retire on a pension, and play golf every day until I drop dead. What fun is that?

If you've been feeling the squeeze of social norms to pick one career and stick with it, I've got good news. And a grenade. So, blow up the unconventional wisdom. What's stopping you from experiencing personal and professional success in one industry after the next? Nothing. In fact, your willingness to do the next thing can save your ass from financial ruin.

In 2011, my life sucked. I found myself in the middle of a divorce. When you're in that state of mind, you're *out* of your mind. At my job in the integrated security systems industry, I wasn't myself. When it was time to move on, I gave myself permission to follow my own advice.

Do the next thing.

At the time, I had been juggling two Beef O'Brady's restaurants in Dayton, Ohio while working in Chicago. Thanks to the one-two sucker punch of the Great Recession and an expensive divorce, I had no idea how to pay my employees. Unemployment reached double digits. Middle class families clipped coupons religiously. Restaurant owners like me saw the writing on the wall. Beginning in 2008, hundreds of Ohio restaurants closed their doors without warning. If either Beef's location could weather the storms of economic downturn, I had to give one of them—and only one of them—*my all*. Sometimes, you just have to stick it out. If I closed both locations, over one hundred jobs would vanish. I couldn't let that happen. So, in the worst market to sell a business since the 1970s, I hung up a For Sale sign and said goodbye to half of my restaurateur dream.

Do the next thing.

Within days, I got a call from my business broker.

"You've got an offer," he said. "A guy who owns a car wash south of town is thinking about a trade. One of your restaurants for his car wash. What do you think?"

I worked for pennies and nickels as a kid helping the attendant at the car wash on the southwest side of Chicago at 87th and California.

"I'm an expert," I said. "Basically. Let's do it. Let's put our attorneys in touch."

Do the next thing.

Two months later, I became the proud owner of a car wash, which, after some tender loving care, has become an even more profitable business. With two businesses to my name at that point, I decided to follow this new stage of my career wherever it led. Integrated security systems sales again? Nope. How about integrated security systems *ownership*?

During the closing stage of the restaurant-car wash swap, I called up an old acquaintance, Tom. He just so happened to own the oldest integrated security systems business in Dayton, Ohio.

"You know, Bill," Tom began after I shared my ambition to get back into systems integration, "I'm starting to think about finally selling this place. It's been a great run, but it's time to retire."

Yes, I was dead-broke at the time, but my banker never forgot my on-time business loan repayments prior to the Recession. After six months of back and forth, we finalized the sale of Copp Integrated Systems. Hello, business number three! Thank God I never paid attention to the posts cluttering my LinkedIn newsfeed about never "being the jack of all trades and master of none." Who says experience in one career or industry can't serve you in another?

I carried my curiosity into the new roles as Owner and CEO. Having the Dayton International Airport as a client put us on the radar of a security sensors developer—and a top-secret U.S. Military project that was ready to become a commercial product.

"You're in the security business. So am I." The developer kicked off a chat over coffee. "Your security systems watch a location to protect both people and property. But what if you could predict when disaster would strike hours before it happened? Anything from petty theft to a terrorist attack."

"No...way!" My initial response probably included an expletive. "How the hell can you predict a crisis before it happens? Wouldn't every military, police force, and sheriff's department on the planet want this?"

The developer's eyes twinkled. "Bingo."

Fifteen minutes of technical explanations and backstory later, my jaw just about touched the floor.

The University of Dayton Research Institute, working with the United States Army and Air Force, had developed a software (later called Footprint) to protect soldiers before, during, and after a battle. It's command and control. The software integrates disparate sensors and data sets, "scans" video and audio recordings, analyzes patterns, and predicts where and when threats will arise.

"I'd like your company to help us commercialize it. Together, Copp and the University of Dayton Research Institute will take Footprint to market and give the power of prediction to every police officer in the world." He leaned over the table and whispered, "*Bill, help us stop crimes before they start.*"

I agreed. We made a deal and scheduled an international tour, showing off Footprint in Nigeria and Dubai. Since then, we've worked with law enforcement and tech entrepreneurs to stop criminals and terrorists before they act.

Do the next thing.

Your career path may not take you from flipping burgers to commercializing software. It doesn't matter. When you're open to trying the next thing, you set yourself up for future success. If I maxed out credit cards to keep *both* restaurants meeting payroll during the Great Recession, where would I be today? Nowhere near the opportunities I've been able to take advantage of, that's for sure.

Whether you're a fifty-something like me or a young gun aiming for that first stable job, keep one eye on the present and one eye on the future. Career success doesn't mean you ride the same wave from college graduation all the way to retirement. The Law of Diminishing Returns states that a point comes when *more* effort produces *fewer* returns.[1] In 2011, I reached the point of Diminishing Returns in integrated systems sales and restaurant ownership. More time, more effort, and more money would've made me broker, quicker.

This Law comes second nature to Millennials. Maybe it's the fact that they've grown up Googling, texting, and web-surfing. Why take an hour to walk to the library for research when saying, "Okay, Google...", "Hey, Siri...", or "Alexa..." takes half a second?

The Millennial spirit is alive and well. Not just in Renaissance Men today like me but in movers and shakers in centuries past. In post-Civil War Virginia, a homemaker named Anna churned butter, canned jams, and sewed quilts to make a living. In that day and age, it wasn't uncommon for half of all children to succumb to disease before age five. Anna herself knew that statistic well—five of her ten babies died before their first birthday. Still, Anna refused to despair. Devoted to her husband and surviving children, she supplemented the family income whenever and however she could. As middle age drew to a close, Anna's arthritis forced her to put down the sewing needle. Her creative outlet, gone.

"But your fingers still work, don't they? Why not pick up a paintbrush?" Her sister suggested. Encouraged, Anna tried her hand at painting nature scenes. These landscapes wound up in town shops, local galleries, regional art fairs and even New York's Museum of Modern Art!

In 2006, Anna "Grandma" Moses' painting *The Sugaring Off* sold for over one million dollars.[2]

Do the next thing.

Almost one hundred years after Grandma Moses was born, an Air Force serviceman contemplated life after the military. Like me, he was a military policeman (MP) stationed in South Korea. While on leave, he meandered into a Korean and Chinese martial arts studio. The self-control and self-discipline required to train appealed to him. The young MP attended classes until honorable discharge from the Air Force. He moved back home to California, opened his own martial arts studio, and took on the Hollywood elite as students. Actors and producers encouraged him to audition for small roles in action films—and he did.

In 1972, *Return of the Dragon* hit theaters, featuring rising martial artist Chuck Norris in a choreographed fight with Bruce Lee.[3]

Do the next thing.

While Chuck Norris trained in South Korea in 1962, an Ohio-born aviator made history. *The first American to orbit earth.* He refused to be the last. Twelve years later, John Glenn was elected United States Senator. Senator Glenn advocated for space exploration, science education, and a more peaceful planet.[4]

Do the next thing.

Anna, Chuck, John, and me—we're all Millennials at heart. If moving on from a career that offers diminishing returns means that I'm "irresponsible" or "entitled," so be it! I'd rather explore. Go on an adventure. *Live life*. With that attitude, nothing can stop you from making your next thing, the best thing. Nothing.

PATCH THE BIGGEST HOLES

The Marines always hit the beach first. In World War II, Marines swarmed island after island, claiming territory for the Allied Powers on their way to victory over a corrupt empire. But they wouldn't have made it past the first sandbar if their Landing Craft Assault boats were riddled with holes. So it is in life. And your career.

Every one of us has opportunities for victory before us, but if we don't patch the holes in our proverbial boats, we'll never get the chance. I define a "hole in the boat" as a skills gap that, left unfilled, will "sink" your career before it ever takes off. Some lack people skills. If they can't make the interviewer feel at ease during chit-chat, for example, that dream job stays out of reach...forever. For others, the skills gap is technical. Sure, they're willing to learn, but potential employers hire competent professionals, not eager students.

From elementary school through college, you're told that learning is the teacher's responsibility. Not yours. No matter what a teacher or professor tells you, only *you* can patch those holes. With a promise of a lucrative profession after graduation, you pick a degree to invest four-plus years of your life earnings. You shell out a few thousand bucks for textbooks... every semester. Then you waste away during class while some professor lectures you for hours on end. You graduate without skills, without job prospects, and without any way of paying back tens of thousands dollars in student loans.

Employers' number-one complaint is that college grads lack practical skills. *Basic* skills colleges never taught.[1] Hiring managers can't fill open jobs because applicants don't meet entry-level requirements! How many open positions are there? More than five and a half million, most of which require *skills*, not a degree.[2] Universities should be ashamed. Instead of selling my future to student loan debtors, I chose to patch my own boat's holes. As a young man, my biggest hole—my widest skills gap—was communication. If you look up the word "proletariat" on Wikipedia, I'm pretty damn sure you'll see a photo from my childhood somewhere on the page. Working class. Blue collar labor. Frugal living. That was me.

The day I joined the Marines, I realized just how far behind my basic communications skills were. At the Marine Recruiting Depot, a First Lieutenant addressed one thousand of us young bucks. Pacing in front of the drill instructors, that tall, fit officer spoke so crisply, so confidently. His eloquence and poise impressed even his superiors. I'm pretty sure he spoke English, but half the words flew right over my head. Words like "ergo," "unscrupulous," and "bifurcated." I dreaded the day we met face to face—and we *would* meet—and he perceived my poor comprehension as insubordination.

After the Marines sent me to North Carolina, my roommate reminded me to patch that hole in my boat. A few yards away from the ocean sat a cool beach house—barely cheap enough for three new Marines to afford together. Somehow we managed to pay rent and still have a few bucks left over for beer at the end of the month. On weekends, we drank, partied, and flirted with the girls who attended our midnight beach bonfires.

One of my Marines roommates was the base writer and photographer Reverge Anselmo, who went on to fight in combat in Lebanon in 1982. After distinguished military service, he wrote several books and produced feature films, such as *Stateside* with Val Kilmer. Just as importantly, Reverge was one hell of a communicator. During late-night, after-party shit shoots, I stammered through "uh's" and "um's" every other word. He spoke with the precision of an ancient Roman orator. During the day, Reverge spent hours reading countless books and sitting in front of his typewriter in the kitchen, writing and honing his communication skills. It's a wonder we even became friends.

"So, uh, why'd you join the Marines?" I asked Reverge one Saturday night after two or three brewskis. "You know, um...to get away from the folks?

Hell, I joined 'cause it's a job. Well, a career, I mean. Being an MP. It's a good career, I think. Uh, you?"

Reverge stared straight ahead, breathing calmly. "I enlisted because my country needs me. And I believe I can help."

I said nothing back. I was dumb as a box of rocks, and we both knew it. But Reverge didn't lord his well-spokenness over me, he let it inspire me. I bought every dictionary, thesaurus, and vocabulary book on the Camp Lejeune bookstore shelves. To make up for lost time, I kept them next to my bunk. First thing every morning and last thing every night, I scoured those books' pages. And whenever Reverge or another Marine used a word I didn't understand, I sounded it out, wrote it down, and looked it up in my books.

Patch the biggest holes.

After the Marines, I took the first job I could, which happened to be an entry-level, unsalaried position. In used car sales. One hundred percent commission. After the third car lot browser in a row jokingly asked me, "You're not gonna screw me over, are you, kid?" I knew my salesmanship needed major improvement. The unparalleled poor reputation of commission-only salespeople certainly didn't help.

Customers needed to trust me *before* they talked to me. So, I invested the remaining dollars of my final Marines paycheck in custom promotional brochures. The front cover displayed a black and white picture of me and the dealership owner shaking hands. The headline read, "Bill DeFries & Bill Jacobs Chevrolet: A Winning Combination."

The printer helped me write snazzy copy about how I, the public's trusted automobile purchase advisor, help shoppers find the right model at the right price. A couple of customer testimonials featured on the brochure back proved my point.

I left stacks of brochures at every doctor's office, library, and grocery store bulletin board within a three-mile radius. Within days, families had to *book an appointment* just to speak with me. Whenever eager customers walked in off the street, they asked for "that handsome gentleman from the brochure." That month, March 1988, I set the dealership record for most cars sold in a single month—thirty-two.

Patch the biggest holes.

I'm not history's only guy to experience explosive success after filling a glaring skills gap. Three years before I enlisted in the United States Marine Corps, a young athlete stared at a handwritten list on the wall of a boy's locker room. His name wasn't on it.

The varsity basketball team needed fifteen players, but fifty kids had attended tryouts. This sophomore kid walked home, closed his bedroom door, and balled his eyes out. That summer, the young baller practiced free throws, three-point shots, and dribbling. Anything close that skills gap. Next season on junior varsity, he *dominated* every second on the floor. He scored forty-plus points in multiple games. More fans showed up to watch JV than varsity!

For the rest of high school, the athlete gave up evenings and weekends to practice. No defender could stop him from making a clutch play. Not in high school, not in college, not in the National Basketball Association.

On June 14th, 1998, Michael Jordan and my hometown Chicago Bulls won their sixth league championship, the only team to "three-peat" twice in American professional basketball history.[3]

Patch the biggest holes.

Michael Jordan followed his hoops passion down a billion-dollar career path. But passion alone is a blind spot that hides the biggest skills gaps. Take a different Michael. While Jordan broke defenders' ankles, another Michael broke wood in carpentry class. This Michael wanted to start a handyman business like his grandfather and set his own hours.

Only one problem. Michael didn't know repair wrap from Saran wrap. His boat didn't just have holes, it had no bottom. Rather than work his ass off to become a mediocre carpenter, Michael decided to level up the skills he *did* have. As a kid, Michael's natural vocal ability earned him spots in the church choir and on high school theatre stages. Giving up shop class opened up Michael's schedule. He practiced, studied choir in college, and graduated with a communications degree. Michael's flair landed him pitchman roles for radio and TV advertisers. Mainstream media producers noticed. When they needed strong male narrators for network documentaries, they called Michael.

On November 7th, 2003, Discovery Channel debuted *Dirty Jobs with Mike Rowe*.[4] From then on, Michael has been a household name among blue collar America.

Patch the biggest holes.

You don't have to be famous to get your shit together like both Michael's did. You certainly won't earn fame if you waste life rowing a sinking boat, much less fortune. Just look at my background. Either skills gap—communication or sales—would've held me back not only on those career paths but on the entrepreneurial road later in life. No way I could've inspired employees at Beef's or have easily built rapport with Copp clients without my biggest holes patched. Even a hole one-eighth of an inch wide sinks the boat eventually. Sooner or later, a skill that takes a few months to learn on your own causes years of frustration if you don't have it.

Ever heard of the Pareto Principle? It's as simple as it is profound—twenty percent of your effort produces eighty percent of your results.[5] In your career, twenty percent of your skills earn eighty percent of your salary, your benefits, and your future opportunities. Only trouble is, we don't know which twenty percent that is! Even so, you can still detect where your skills gaps are. So, find them. Patch them. Before it's too late.

WEAR YOUR BADGES

I like fruit salad. No, I don't mean the kind with marshmallows. That's what we call the collection of service ribbons and medals on a military uniform. These badges are public reminders of bravery, good conduct, or participation in a battle or campaign. Whenever I wore my dress blues in the Marines on base or off, I displayed my own badges—on the left side of my chest, right below the collarbone, all in a row. Recognition for my accomplishments, reminders to achieve even more.

Since October 10th, 1775, Marines have held themselves to a standard of excellence that makes them the most esteemed branch of America's armed forces. From first Marine Samuel Nicholas to the most decorated Marine Chesty Puller, every Marine knows their worth.

My own badges earned respect from superiors and respect from me...*for myself.* I esteemed myself according to my accomplishments. Compare that to the usual definition of self-esteem, a subjective feeling about your own worth that may or may not be accurate.

I believe people deserve respect based on what they've accomplished. But it's easy for most of us to forget those accomplishments. When difficult times roll into life like a bad storm, keep yourself afloat. Wear your badges. Wear them proudly. If your career badges are as simple as a GED or high school diploma, wear them! Frame them and hang them on your wall. Take pride in those badges. Starve self-doubt with reminders of everything you've already accomplished in your career. This builds up the confidence to accomplish even more. It's a self-perpetuating cycle, a self-fulfilling prophecy. You, with your badges displayed for the world to see, are a prophecy of success that causes itself to come to pass.

For example, as a youngster, I subscribed to *Gentleman's Quarterly*. My favorite sections weren't the stories, they were the ads. I used to tear out the advertisements of powerful men in perfectly tailored business suits with their briefcases in tow. These pictures etched into my mind the image of success—"mad men" who could do anything and be anything, who wheeled-and-dealed with class. That was a badge I wanted to wear.

While stationed in South Korea, I visited a tailor in Seoul and bought myself two hand-tailored suits. The tailor worked the fabric around my body just right and even monogrammed my name—"William E. DeFries"—

into the jacket. After my honorable discharge, I hit the streets of suburban Chicago. My very first sales gig lasted ten days before the place shut down. With a wife, a home, and bills to pay, I was desperate for something, anything. But I didn't act like it. Instead, I bought a burgundy leather briefcase with gold locks for twenty bucks at an auction to pair with my suits.

First thing next Monday morning, I put on my gray hand-tailored suit, grabbed my empty briefcase, and walked the streets. Unemployed yet invincible. My prophecy of success fulfilled itself at the end of the first interview.

"Can you start today?" Jerry Mutz, general sales manager of Bill Jacobs Chevrolet asked me. Of course I agreed. Within one year, I set the all-time dealership record for most vehicles sold in a single month.

Wear your badges.

Five years later, my prodigy-like sales success flat-lined. There my butt sat in a plain black office chair at a plain white desk. Promotions took me away from the customers. Management gave me hours of paperwork. Every day. I hated it.

On one plain afternoon on a plain day during a plain week, an usual customer caught my eye on my lunch break. A psychologist. She carried a stack of pamphlets that talked about "affirmations" and "life coaching." This was 1987. Nobody back then had ever heard of affirmations or life coaching! Our casual chat in the car lot turned into a booked consultation. Then three appointments.

Yes, I thought it was hokie. Yes, I thought I might be getting scammed. But the psychologist taught me about short-range and long-range goals, which I'd never thought about before. My wife and I had two young daughters now. Wasn't my goal to provide for them good enough? During each appointment, the psychologist played a cassette tape of affirmations. I don't remember a single one, but I do remember the homework she asked me to complete during the week.

"Answer these questions: your personal and professional accomplishments, your dreams for the future, and an inventory of your skills."

That homework was harder than any homework I'd ever attempted before, including that one semester of community college I never finished. Whatever the hell I turned in deserved a failing grade. The psychologist told me, "Every goal you wrote about is about someone else. You want to give your family a wonderful house, great schools, nice vacations. You want to be all you can be for them. What about yourself?"

Her question was a watershed moment for me. Never had I organized my life around what I wanted to do or where I wanted to go. I tried the homework again. It felt better this time. Putting my thoughts on the page made my goals real, tangible. When I made an inventory of my skills and a list of my accomplishments, I felt like a total badass. I converted that homework assignment into a habit. Whenever the public recognizes a good deed I've done for the community, I include a memento in my inventory. Today, my inventory is my office. Four walls, three sets of shelves, and two desks display newspaper clippings, awards and trophies, photo ops, and thank you notes. All reminders I can achieve any goal I set my mind and heart to. Now, whenever I face a new struggle, and I'm tempted to drop my head in despair, I go into my office and look around.

Wear your badges.

My decision to collect concrete reminders of accomplishments resulted from a chance encounter. I'm not the only atypically successful person to wear a badge I hadn't expected. While I stirred up trouble on the streets of Chicago's south side as a kid, a Pennsylvania boy chose entrepreneurship over juvenile delinquency. Mark, the descendant of immigrants, wanted to live by his own rules and make his own way in the world. That meant buying what he wanted, whenever he wanted. His first love—a pair of shoes with a price tag beyond his middle class family's budget.

So, Mark looked for opportunities to make a profit. At age twelve, he went door to door selling, of all things, garbage bags. Neighbors' spare pocket change added up to more than the shoes' price. That wasn't the end of his sales career, merely the beginning. As a teenager, he bought stamps and coins, then resold them for an even greater profit. To pad his college fund, Mark taught himself dance theory, then turned around and gave dance lessons to fellow students.

Meanwhile, emerging technologies helped companies all over America switch from typewriters to computers. To keep up, Mark taught himself computer networking and worked his way up the tech career ladder. Mark's work ethic attracted a buyer for his first startup, a six million-dollar sale, then a buyer for his second startup—a six *billion*-dollar sale. Mark Cuban re-invested his fortune and bought the Dallas Mavericks professional basketball franchise.[1]

Wear your badges.

But not all success stories end "profitably ever after." History proves that some badges are admired only after they're despised. More than a century before Mark bought the basketball team, an orphaned New York socialite saw little hope for her own future. Nicknamed "Granny" for her attitude and plain appearance, Anna threw herself into her schoolwork. In that era, women knew their place. But Anna refused to accept it.

She traveled to Europe and received a progressive education. Even after marriage and children entered the picture, Anna kept her dream to enter public service alive. When her youngest child reached toddlerhood, Anna entered politics. She campaigned for a local gubernatorial candidate, then for her own causes. Sexist stereotypes couldn't silence her. Anna spoke and wrote in favor of both civil rights and human rights to whoever listened.

After World War II, Anna Eleanor Roosevelt accepted a presidential appointment to the United Nations. She chaired the Commission on Human Rights and co-authored the Universal Declaration of Human Rights.[2]

Wear your badges.

Mark Cuban, Eleanor Roosevelt, and I may have very little in common. I'm not a billionaire, and I'm no longer a Democrat. But each of us has worn our badges proudly and earned the respect of others—and ourselves—as a result. I don't care if your badges are a suit and tie, a billion-dollar fortune, or a groundbreaking political career. The first person you need to believe in yourself is you. So, gather up your own badges. Make a list of your accomplishments. Look at yourself in the mirror with pride.

You *can* do great things in this world. Because you already have.

PLAN WHEN OTHERS WING IT

"Have your ducks in a row."

When I was a kid, my Dad used to say that after I told him about my next too-big-for-my-britches idea, ambition, or dream. I never knew what he meant. Until I studied ducks. Ducklings' tendency to follow mom in a straight line during the day's web-footed travels is an ancient evolved trait.[1] Any duckling straying out of line toward danger becomes nature's fast food for nearby predators. Ducklings' organized forward movement is a way to minimize risk. I can't think of a better metaphor for this than Due Diligence, the process of evaluating all the risks associated with a goal.[2]

If your mind is set on an outside-the-box career, then by definition, you're taking a risk. You're out in the wild like a duck with its babies. Without Due Diligence, you'll allow your future to be gobbled up by predators and competitors. So, when others "wing" it and stray from the risk-mitigated path, plan. Be the person who plans so well that your chance of success is higher than anyone expects. Even you. Like a great military strategist, you'll know where the greatest risks lie in wait, those threats that doom your dreams to remain dreams. When you can accept every risk fully, that's your confirmation—the plan's ready.

But it's not enough to discuss risk in theory. Risks are never abstract. They get under your collar. They breathe down your neck. They whisper in your ear at night, haunting your sleep. I know a thing or two about risk. In the late 1980s, I felt like a high roller. My sales job at Bill Jacobs Chevrolet offered a six-figure salary, which already made me a success. But I wanted more. Something different, at least. The next step on my atypical path called—professional acting.

Now or never.

It may have been stupid to sacrifice a six-figure salary with a wife, two children, a mortgage, two car payments, and two private school tuitions. But I mitigated the risk—and the stupidity—with a comprehensive plan. I bought a leather-bound journal and wrote down every obstacle between me and my first paying gig. No professional training, no agent, no headshot, no scheduled auditions, no memorized monologue. Before I wrote my own pink slip, I checked things off this list.

Once I landed auditions, I wrote each casting director's feedback in my journal. "Too quiet. Not enough 'oomph,'" some said. "Project more. Make me feel the emotion."

I also tracked my success to failure ratio. Out of my first five auditions, I landed two roles.

What do these two roles have in common? I wrote in my journal. *Audition for more of THAT!*

My ratio improved. Casting directors referred me to their peers. My agent booked higher-paying auditions with less competition. Two months into my career transition, nine out of the ten aspiring actors I met at the headshot photographer's studio had quit acting. Meanwhile, my first paycheck showed up in the mail.

Plan when others wing it.

Eleven years later, I entered a different industry, restaurants. Franchises in particular. Beef O'Brady's specifically. After decades of working jobs for others, I wanted to be a job creator. A single restaurant employs up to fifty people, so why not start there? Back to rookie status again.

I took the biggest risks a middle-aged guy can. I withdrew my 401(k)—my entire retirement nest egg—and paid that damn twenty percent tax penalty. I signed over my home and life insurance policies to personally guarantee loan repayment. If I failed, I would lose literally everything. My family wouldn't even have a van to live in down by the river! Ninety percent of restaurants fail in the first year. How crazy did I have to be?

Crazy enough to mitigate those risks, for one. Ten months before deciding which franchisor to purchase a license from, I started on my business plan. No way I'd sacrifice my family's well-being without knowing what the hell I was getting myself into! So, I did my homework. I drove through neighborhoods, counted playground sets in backyards, and walked the streets to get a feel of my future patrons.

Thirty-seven pages of market research, revenue projections, and advertising plans later, I was ready. The day my first Beef O'Brady's location opened in 2004, everything went according to plan. All those Sundays watching Chicago Bears football players "block and tackle" on the field as a kid paid off. I coached my new employees like players on a scoring drive. I had a saying—"On time is ten minutes before your shift starts." Everyone had to make their shift on time, no second chances. Every meal had to be right. And every customer had to leave with a smile on their face, or we counted their business lost. I wanted this dining to be more than a meal, I wanted customers to experience an "event" and have them walking out thinking, *Wow, that was cool.*

One full year after opening, Beef O'Brady's Corporate recognized me as Rookie of the Year at a romantic resort in Tampa Bay, Florida. My first Beef's franchise raked in so much profit, I paid back business loans, paid off both car payments, and made triple mortgage payments. Most importantly, the restaurant made a difference in the Miami Valley. Among thirty-seven pages of business plans, I charted course toward a revolutionary new way to advertise. Today, no restaurant, much less local business, meets payroll without it. I called the idea "cause-related marketing." I approached academic and athletic organizations with this win-win fundraising opportunity. On the day of their choosing, I would donate a percentage of all profit from the day's sales at Beef's to their cause. My mission? Support and promote academic and athletic excellence among families in Dayton. Together, our organizations would market the event in the weeks leading up to guarantee a high turnout. The restaurant saw *ten times* the usual foot traffic on the selected fundraising day. The nonprofit leveraged the additional funding to change individuals' lives for the better.

Plan when others wing it.

Whether you want to change the world or change your chances of paying off that student loan on time, know what the hell you're doing first. Look for risks, evaluate each risk, and plan for each risk. Like I did. Like a guy named Jeffrey Jorgensen did.

The same year my McDonald's commercial debuted on national TV, Jeffrey drew up his own plans to mitigate risks. The internet was just a few weeks old. Personal computer purchases skyrocketed. America Online mailed unsolicited discs to millions of Americans to increase world wide web usage using the AOL browser. Based on the number of people installing that and other browsers, internet use was on track to grow by over two thousand percent every year.

While nursing a budding career in the stock market, Jeffrey couldn't take his eyes off the opportunity that was the internet. Maybe he could launch the world's first online store. He researched products, narrowed down his list, and presented his business plan to potential investors—mom and dad.

"A thirty percent chance of success." Jeffrey admitted.

Good enough. His confidence in the business plan and his parents' confidence in their son made his idea into reality. Within two months of launch, Jeffrey's website saw over twenty *thousand* dollars' worth of product move every single week.

Five years later, Jeffrey—now known by his stepfather's last name, Bezos—was named *TIME* Person of the Year. He'd turned personal computers into shopping carts through his ecommerce retailer, AMAZON.com.[3]

Plan when others wing it.

One of the riskiest moves an aspiring entrepreneur can make is working without a net—quitting the current job before creating a new one. That's why Jeff evaluated different products to sell before leaving Wall Street. It's also why I worked full-time while researching Beef O'Brady's. I worked very long hours, but it was easy because I had a purpose. (I resigned my General Manager position once I was one hundred percent sure.)

In some cases, that overlap of new career and old career lasts *years*. The more thorough the plan, the fewer the risks, the higher chance of success. A fax machine salesperson named Sara had no problem investing time in Due Diligence. For two years, she worked on her business idea. She researched patents, roamed competitors' stores for ideas, and built relationships with suppliers.

Any outside-the-box career move is risky, especially an entrepreneurial one. Only after Sara believed her business could make it did she quit the nine-to-five, and even then, only after it turned a profit! Two weeks before appearing on *The Oprah Winfrey* Show to showcase her hot new hosiery products, SPANX founder Sara Blakely quit her day job.[4]

Plan when others wing it.

Whether you're a normal guy like me, the world's richest man, or a working parent with a big dream, atypical success IS possible. If you know your risks. If you know them like your best friend and worst enemy. If you know exactly what you're getting into, where things could go to hell in grandma's handbasket, and how you'll make sure they don't. Because success requires risks. So, accept them. Plan. Then succeed.

STAND UP NO MATTER WHAT

The date: September 5th, 1918.
The place: Comiskey Park, Chicago, Illinois.
The event: the World Series.

Nobody felt like celebrating. News of American Marines and soldiers killed in World War I bled through every newspaper headline in town. Fewer than twenty thousand people attended game one of the World Series, the lowest turnout in history. Halfway through the game, the crowd was so quiet, players could barely tell there even *was* a crowd.

Then something...*special* happened. During a break in the seventh inning, a Navy band substituted patriotism for the usual entertainment. As the first notes of "The Star Spangled Banner" left their instruments, fans and players stood. They took off their hats, faced the flagpole, and sang the National Anthem together. One player, Red Sox infielder Fred Thomas, a Navy veteran, stood at attention and saluted the flag.

This gesture earned more whistles and cheers from the crowd than a walk-off home run.[1]

Fifty years later, I stood in those same bleachers at Comiskey Park for White Sox games with my father. When the speakers blared, "*O say, can you see, by the dawn's early light...*" before each game, my dad belted out the National Anthem. In those days, men just didn't sing. Sure, we had crooners like Dean Martin or Frank Sinatra, but unless a guy was in church, he didn't sing—with that one exception. My dad always stood for the National Anthem at sporting events and sang along with the enthusiasm of a Christmas caroler.

It wasn't until I enlisted in the Marine Corps that I realized what the National Anthem and Flag meant to my father. The public playing of the National Anthem is the one moment in time when Americans of every race, color, and creed come together. We honor our heritage of "Life, Liberty and the pursuit of Happiness" and remember those who've died in our defense. As a Marine, I was willing to lay down my life fighting under the Flag if duty called me. Every Marine I served with— man or woman, white or black, citizen or immigrant— feels that way.

Fast forward from my childhood at the ballpark and my twenties as a serviceman to my entrepreneurial days. In the 2000s and 2010s, I rode my Beef O' Brady's Rookie of the Year momentum year after year. Together, we battled through the Great Recession, retained our customer base, and came out stronger than ever. I loved my patrons, and my patrons loved my sports bar.

Then duty called. Ninety-nine years after American sports built a platform to celebrate the Flag and National Anthem, that platform collapsed. In September 2017, Beef's staff turned on the TVs for opening week of the National Football League season. We watched, horrified, as athletes kneeled during the playing of the National Anthem. As a Veteran, I felt disrespected. Personally attacked. I wasn't alone.

"It's not good," I told my general manager over the phone. "Veterans all over are burning NFL memorabilia and demanding cable refunds. I want to change the channel on Beef's TVs, but most people expect football."

"I stand behind you one hundred percent," my GM said. "We're hearing the same thing from customers, especially the Veterans. So, what do you want to do?"

I didn't have an answer, not immediately. Maybe some of the athletes had a reason to protest, a good reason even. Did I want them to get yanked off the field or lose their jobs? No, it's a free country after all, and Marines are willing to die to protect that freedom.

The more I thought about the football players' kneeling, the more I realized I couldn't do *nothing*. I weighed my options based on an ethical principle I read about during a binge-reading session in the Marines. According to Consequential Theory, the right thing to do is whatever action leads to more good than evil.[2]

"I can't stop the players from exercising their free speech rights," I said to my staff during an impromptu meeting. "But I won't stop myself from exercising mine. Until NFL players end their disrespect of the National Anthem and American Flag, we're not going to show NFL games at Beef's anymore." I paused to see my employees' response—mostly nods of agreement. "My stance might hurt business. No, it *will* hurt business. But it's the right thing to do. Don't worry, I'm going to cover any tip shortfalls. I'm going to take care of you."

Next, I ordered wall-sized banners to hang up inside and outside the restaurant to make my stance clear to patrons. Next to the crossed-out letters "NFL" on the banners were four words I expected to doom the restaurant:

"We Stand For America."

During lunch, I typed out my reasoning for the pro-National Anthem stance and published my thoughts on Beef's social media profiles.

"Give it a month," I said aloud to myself after the post went live, "and our doors are shut."

That afternoon, Beef's phones rang off the hook.

"Thank you for standing up for Veterans. Thank you for standing up for what you believe in," one caller after the next said.

By noon, word of the "We Stand For America" banners reached every local media outlet. Newscasters camped out in the parking lot with cameras and mics. Bloggers, podcasters, and commentators broadcast the story to tens of millions of Americans.

The next Sunday, customers waited *four hours* for an open table. Letters from all over the United States piled up on my desk. Heartfelt notes of appreciation for reminding the world why we honor the National Anthem and American Flag. Then the donations came. Dozens of checks showed up at the restaurant and my office from fellow Vets. They wanted to grow the Beef's employee scholarship fund—we didn't even *have* a scholarship fund! I never expected an outpouring of support, especially not at the height of football season. In the Marines, I was willing to sacrifice my life to protect my country. As owner of Beef O'Brady's, I was willing to sacrifice my profits to follow my moral compass.

Stand up no matter what.

The fall of 2017 wasn't the first time I stood up and risked everything. More than ten years prior, I put myself directly in the crosshairs of Centerville business owners. At the time, every restaurant, bar, and public facility in Ohio had smoking and non-smoking sections. I hated it. My mom was a chain smoker. As a boy, I pleaded with her to throw those cigarettes away. More than once secondhand smoke choked me out of the house. She died at age fifty-four of lung cancer.

Since her funeral, I thought of her every time I caught a whiff of cigarette smoke. On airplanes. At the bowling alley. In restaurants. When my girls were young, I'd take the family out to eat at local restaurants after church.

"Smoking or non-smoking?" The first question out of the host's mouth.

"The non-smoking section has a forty-five minute wait," he'd say. "But plenty of smoking section tables are available. No wait."

Whenever I took the risk, I regretted it. Our hair, clothes, and—later that day—the entire *house* reeked of my mother's killer.

After my first Beef O'Brady's opened to record-setting success, I took a stand. Two years before I even opened, I decided my restaurant would be a one hundred percent non-smoking family sports bar and grill.

"We're going to be the first sports bar in Ohio to ban smoking," I announced my policy to city council. "Approve construction of my new restaurant, and families will have a safe and *healthy* place to enjoy a meal together."

A reporter in the audience took detailed notes, and the story ended up in *The Dayton Daily News*. I didn't ask permission from Beef's corporate first. I didn't ask for forgiveness either.

"Mr. DeFries, we strongly advise you to reconsider this...*idea* of yours," a Beef's corporate representative called me after *The Dayton Daily News* syndicated the story. "Alcohol sales are the backbone of every franchise. People want to drink beer and smoke cigarettes. Period."

"I know this market. You don't." I shot back. "My customer base is a mom with a five year-old Little

Leaguer. She drinks diet Coke, and he eats mac and cheese. Period. Smoking hurt my family. I won't have that in my restaurant. Period."

"Then your alcohol, beer, and wine and overall sales will not be what you expect."

Turns out, the guy at corporate was right. Sales weren't what I expected. They *rose*. By thirty percent. The American Heart and Lung Association even mentioned our restaurant in a story. Out-of-state sports leagues came to Beef's *because* we were non-smoking. They sought me out to thank me personally.

Eight months later, the city of Centerville announced an ordinance for city council to decide— ban smoking inside all restaurants, bars, and bowling alleys. All dining establishments, really.

"Look at that Bill DeFries," pro-ordinance councilmen and women said in the lead up to the vote. "If he can pull off a smoking ban, so can everyone else in town."

Sales soared over the summer and rose *again* in the fall. One week before the city council voted on the ordinance, the owner of the bowling alley next door dropped into Beef's.

"Bill." He strolled up to the bar. "Can I talk to you for a second?"

"Sure." I peeled away from a chat with my general manager. "What can I do for you?"

"So, uh..." He shifted weight foot to foot. "Well, me and some concerned bar and restaurant owners in town was wondering if we could get your advice on something. On this *ordinance*," he whispered. "Can you drop by after dinner shift? Say, 'round eight?"

I glanced at the clock. "My pleasure. Glad to help out my fellow entrepreneurs. See you at eight."

"Great. Okay. Good. Well..." He was standing close enough to shake my hand. He didn't. He waved at me. "See ya."

I turned back to my GM and picked up where we left off. We whizzed through dinner, and I finished some paperwork in my office. At five till, I rolled down my sleeves and walked across the parking lot. Cigarette smoke filled my nostrils before I got to the bowling alley entrance. *Thank God this is about to be over.* I believed in city council.

I walked past the vending machines and saw the owner standing in front of the birthday party room. Arms crossed high over his chest.

"Hey!" I waved.

A deadpan look.

Okay...

I offered a handshake. He accepted.

"So, what do you all—" I stepped into the party room. Ten restaurant and bar owner-operators standing in a circle. Silence. Angry stares. Cigarette smoke so thick I coughed twice.

"Have a seat, Mr. DeFries," the bowling alley owner told me. We'd always been on a first name basis.

"I heard you gentlemen have questions about implementing a non-smoking policy in your bars and restaurants."

The group broke into throaty, phlegmy laughter. "You bet we do." Somebody hacked.

I pulled back the yellowed upholstered chair, but I didn't sit.

"You want the truth?" the alley owner asked. He stepped around me to join his gang. "The truth is, your little stunt is going to hurt our business. Government's got no right coming in here telling us private businessmen what we can and cannot do."

"I have nothing to do with the ordinance," I said. "My sports bar smoking ban was my decision. I don't want my customers and employees to have to go home smelling like ashtrays."

"You don't know what you're doing," someone else said. "Big mistake."

"You're a rookie. You're new at this," said another. "You got lucky. You had a great opening. It's the honeymoon, and it's going to be over."

"And it *will* be over," the bowling alley owner said. "You can be damn sure about that." Everyone nodded slowly.

A threat. So classy.

"Nice setup, guys. I have nothing else to say." I walked out.

The ordinance passed. The following November, Ohio banned smoking in all restaurants and bars. Some of those businesses shut down. Several more paid tens of thousands in fines because they ignored the ordinance. Fourteen years later, the Beef O'Brady's honeymoon continues.

Stand up no matter what.

Despite the National Anthem naysayers or restaurant threats, I worried only about Beef's and my employees, not my own life. Back on the baseball field, another man who took a stance faced death threats. Before Civil Rights, racists subjected their African-American neighbors to abuse, discrimination, and hate. Racism prevented competent, worthy black men and women from roles they'd rightfully earned. The injustice was clear, especially in sports. But one feisty baseball manager bridged the racial divide and brought healing to a nation.

After a newspaper quoted the manager on his desire to hire a black player, the major league commissioner demanded a retraction. He refused. When rumors of the manager's intention to follow through spread, several star players on his team demanded a trade. To address the racists on his team, the manager called a midnight meeting and laid down the law—no matter what color their new player was, he'd play. The manager already had a player in mind.

Six days before the 1947 baseball season, manager Leo Durocher made good on his commitment to racial equality. The Los Angeles Dodgers signed Jackie Robinson. Racists in broadcasting and in opposing teams' dugouts hurled epithets and death threats. But Durocher united the team around the league's first African-American superstar.[3]

Stand up no matter what.

Injustice prevails only as long as good people allow. It doesn't matter where. In restaurants, on the playing field, or in a foreign country. In the early 1980s, a former teacher and freelance writer named David stood up for those who couldn't.

On assignment in Latin America for a new employer, David covered Cuba, Mexico, as well as Nicaragua, where socialist thugs tortured and murdered thousands of people on their way to power.[4]

During one of his many travels, David befriended human rights lawyer named Roger Guevara, himself a torture victim of the socialist *Sandinistas*. While advocating for Roger's release for an unjust prison sentence, David met a single mother named Marta Celia. When David discovered Nicaragua's jackboots tailing Marta and seven year-old son Felipe around town, he knew it was a matter of time before they joined Roger in a dark cell.

David made contact with Costa Rica's foreign minister and arranged for Marta and Felipe's escape under cover of darkness. The trip went off hitch-free, David met them on the runway, and together, they escaped back to David's home in New York. Any guess what happened next? David proposed. Marta said yes.

A few years later, David's bold on-site reporting landed him an invitation to sit between news media moguls Rupert Murdoch and Roger Ailes. The two men bragged about their fledgling cable network called Fox News Channel.

"How would you like a full time job on television?" Roger asked David.[5]

It took a year, but David finally accepted. Since then, David Asman has been a mainstay of Fox News and Fox Business Network, interviewing presidents, prime ministers, and pop culture icons.[6] (Between all the big names, David found a spot to interview me when I stood up for America and took on the NFL.)

Stand up no matter what.

Whether you're standing up for Veterans or standing up to racists, taking a controversial stance isn't difficult. Accepting the *consequences* of the decision—that's the hard part. Throughout your atypical career, opportunities to take a stand will cross your path. An injustice won't sit well with you. Corruption will turn your stomach. A disrespectful act will keep you up at night. Atypical success requires atypical action, even if taking a stance risks your reputation, your business, or career. Standing up no matter what has nothing to do with climbing the career ladder and everything to do with protecting your integrity. Without integrity, you've got nothing.

Nothing.

So, when the athletes kneel and the racists hurl insults, will you be true to yourself? Will you follow your moral compass? Will you do the right thing?

Will you stand up no matter what?

GIVE, DON'T GIVE BACK

"I think you're going to love our new initiative," the young filmmaker seated across from me said.

"It's all about bringing awareness to problems in the community, and that's really important," said his wife, a candidate in a local election.

"I like it," I said. "Let's roll up our sleeves together. How can I help?"

"Well," the filmmaker scratched his beard, "we believe in giving back, so—"

"Hold up." I raised my palm.

"What?" they both said.

"Why would I give back to the community? I didn't take anything."

Shock fell off their faces, replaced by the look you have when you get an inside joke. "That's...that's *right*," the young candidate nodded, "we haven't taken anything. We're here to *give*."

"Just give. Don't give back." I smiled. "You never stole anything in the first place."

"You should write that down," the filmmaker said. I agree.

&&&&

Philanthropy isn't just for rich people. It's for people with a purpose who want to get ahead. On your journey to atypical success, opportunities for a better job, higher pay, and wiser mentors will cross your path. Most of them will pass you by. You might not even notice them. But there they are, waiting to be opened and leveraged. To claim those opportunities, give. Just give. Be generous with your time and your treasure, not out of obligation or guilt, but out of Self-Interest.[1]

Self-Interest is *not* the same as being *selfish*. Selfish people take. Self-*interested* people give. As a result, they receive more in return than they ever expected. This isn't just my opinion, it's a principle first taught by the father of economics, Adam Smith. In 1776, Smith published *The Wealth of Nations*. He believed that when people act in their Self-Interest, they create value for others and receive value in return.

That's how I run Beef O'Brady's—and have since the beginning. Less than a year into the business, I sponsored twenty Little League baseball teams. As a youngster in Chicago, I learned how to make friends, how to compete fairly, how to be a good sport, how to be a team player, how to contribute as an individual, and how to handle defeat gracefully all on the baseball diamond. If I can help fund the same character-building experience for the next generation, why wouldn't I?

To celebrate Beef's first year in business and announce the Little League sponsorships, my staff arranged a slot in our local Fourth of July parade. One of the coaches led a troop of fifty kids, all in orange Beef's sponsored uniforms, in his orange '57 Chevy. A photo of us hangs in my office to this day.

I funded thousands of boys' Little League dreams because I wanted to. Not because I felt guilty or obligated. I gave, and the world gave back to *me*. After every game, minivan caravans migrated from the baseball fields to Beef O'Brady's. Coaches kept the bar busy. Players posed for photos with servers. Parents tipped well.

Three years later when the economy fell off a cliff, I never expected those Little League families to be the ones to save Beef's from going out of business. But that's exactly what happened. On the days when two people showed up for lunch, we knew we could count on those minivans to bring us the six o'clock rush. Little Leaguers' word-of-mouth marketing sent enough customers our way to play another inning.

Give, don't give back.

Self-Interest led me into Little League sponsorship, but sometimes, the opportunities come *to you*. Before writing a book shifted from pipe dream to possibility in my mind, my niece Carly invited me to speak to students at her school. (Carly is a high school counselor across from Marquette Park on Chicago's southwest side.)

"Uncle Billy, you can be a positive influence," Carly said. "When I look at you, somebody who goofed off in school, who didn't go to college, who caused a lot of trouble...I see several of my students. Most are hard-working, ambitious, and motivated to succeed. But those who aren't? They have to believe they have a future. You can be that future."

I wish I'd consulted Self-Interest, because I said no. Repeatedly. For two years. Then on the eve of an impromptu Chicago trip with my fiancé Lorie, I had a change of heart and called Carly.

"Tell you what, I'll throw some slides together and speak to your kids for, say, twenty minutes? Thirty?"

"YES!" Carly squealed. "You have no idea how much you're going to mean to these kids. NO idea!"

I really didn't. That night, I scanned old black and white photos from my childhood and uploaded them into a blank PowerPoint template. From the Marines to McDonald's commercials, I documented every step on my atypical career path. From eager troublemaker to entrepreneur.

"I can't believe this is me," I told Lorie. "I should be working on a loading dock somewhere. A bad back, no savings, a criminal record..."

"Don't forget bad teeth." Lorie chuckled.

"I should be a nobody. But somehow, I'm not." I deleted my name off the first slide and hit save on my makeshift presentation.

The next morning, Lorie, her teenage son, my youngest daughter, and her husband followed me into the high school. Carly met us at the administrative office.

"Carly told us all about you," another counselor said, shaking my hand. "I have high hopes for your talk."

"I'll try to live up to them."

Family and staff exchanged greetings, I handed Carly my flash drive, and we set up in the largest classroom at the school. While Carly and I tested the projector, thirty kids, none of whom looked like me, took seats. At the back, my family represented the standing room only section. I buttoned my navy blue jacket and clicked my first slide.

"The Atypical Career Path to Success," I read off the displayed slide. "I'm going to tell you all a story. A story about a boy from the south side of Chicago."

Slide after slide, I told the story without revealing the protagonist's name. Quitting the teamster job, stealing my parents' car, getting kicked out of home, flunking college. Juniors and seniors nodded—they saw themselves in these slides. Their siblings. Their friends. Then my story took a few turns—into the armed forces, sales, television commercials, and theatrical productions.

"Nobody expected this kid to go anywhere. He wasn't born with a silver spoon in his mouth, he didn't get any handouts, and he didn't take school seriously. When he started applying himself in sports, that's when he really showed up. That's when he took himself seriously." My slide showed high school Bill posing for baseball and football team photos. "He wishes he would've stayed in school and applied himself, too. All that success he had would've come a lot sooner. I know he wishes that. Because he...is *me.*"

Every student looked surprised. Except one. A broad-shouldered boy in the front row. A handsome young man. Paper thin moustache. Probably a senior. Probably an athlete. He raised his hand.

"Yes?"

He crossed his arms over his desk. "Why was football important to you?"

"Because it was hard." The words came out before I thought about them. My family laughed awkwardly. "Seriously. It was tough. The coaches drove us to be physically and mentally fit. There were lots of times I wanted to quit. But I didn't quit. In the end, it was worth it. I forged my future on the football field. I've made a lot of mistakes, but I'm not a quitter."

"Cool," he said quietly. "I was curious 'cause I'm on the football team here."

"That's great. Don't dread those practices and drills. Sticking with them is the keystone of your future."

With that, Carly called the end of the class.

"Dad, that was awesome!" My daughter threw her arms around me as students filed out.

"Yes!" Carly agreed. "Thank you for sharing your story."

"Feels good to give," I said. "Who was that kid in the front row? He plays football here?"

Carly's joy faded. "Actually, he's one of the reasons I've been asking you to come here." We stood behind the teacher's desk. "In his freshman year, Jamal got caught with a handgun. Around here, firearms violations are like membership cards for the gangs. All his friends dropped out, and they run drugs a few blocks from here. They're trying to pull him into their world. But he's a good kid with a lot of promise. You were a troubled kid, too. I thought if he could see that you made it in life, he'd see he can, too."

Give, don't give back.

Since my talk that day, Jamal's chances have improved thanks to another former Chicago south sider. Growing up surrounded by drugs, guns, and crime, a boy named Jonathan dreamed of getting the hell out of there and finding fame and fortune. And he did. But like my heart for the baseball diamond and the football field, Jonathan's heart for his old neighborhood sent him on a mission.

On May 27th, 2014, Jonathan put his stage name—Chance the Rapper—and social media platform to work. He pleaded with kids like Jamal to put down their guns. They listened. In a city that averages a half-dozen shootings *per day*, no gunshots were heard for two days straight. After the streak, President Barack Obama invited Chance to a VIP round table to promote justice and peace in African-American communities.[2] Since then, Chance pledged a one million dollar donation to Chicago mental health services.[3]

Give, don't give back.

Other entertainers joined the urban giving list alongside Chance the Rapper. Basketball superstar (and alumnus of my high school) Dwayne Wade runs after-school programs that keeps kids off the south side streets.[4] Two states over in Ohio, LeBron James opened a charter school for at-risk third and fourth-graders. The school offers job placement services to students' parents *and* guarantees university scholarships.[5]

But you don't have to win Grammys, help underprivileged kids, or open restaurants to add value that repays you in ways you can't even imagine. Another Illinoisan followed his own Self-Interest compass through young adulthood and beyond.

The third of fourteen children, a boy named Daniel felt invisible. Surrounded by older, smarter, and taller kids at home and at school. Dyslexia, a common reading disorder, held him back. When he finally squeaked his way through high school, he joined the United States Navy. At the height of the Vietnam war, Daniel served not one second in combat. He was a paper-pusher whose greatest battlefield glory was sharpening pencils. Two years of active duty, and Daniel opted for civilian work, then college.

In those days, any student could try out for college athletics. At football tryouts, Daniel pushed himself as hard as out-of-state recruits riding full scholarships.

The coach saw Daniel's potential and gave him a shot. On the practice squad. There Daniel made no name for himself. During games, Daniel haunted the sidelines, barely noticeable among superstar players a foot taller and twice his weight. Sorting erasers and staples in the hull of a ship felt more meaningful.

But Daniel's moxie didn't got *completely* unnoticed. During the last home game of the season, the coach searched the sidelines for little Daniel.

"Defensive end," the coach said, the position Daniel was to play.

"Yes I can!" Daniel scurried off the sidelines and into the game. Three plays later, Daniel "Rudy" Ruettiger sacked the quarterback. His teammates carried him off the field on their shoulders, chanting, "*RU-DY, RU-DY!*"[6]

Rudy didn't let campus game or the blockbuster film made about his life get to his head..[7] After graduating from Notre Dame, he co-founded the Rudy Foundation, a nonprofit that awards scholarships to student athletes who exhibit the same underdog determination and quiet strength that earned Rudy a spot on the field of play.[8]

Twenty years before I studied improv comedy at Second City in Chicago, another William took to the theatre company's stage. Growing up north of Chicago, this William didn't go into show business alone. Together with three of his five brothers, William joked, wrote, and acted his way to stardom.

Multiple Academy, Emmy, and Golden Globe Award wins and nominations later, Bill Murray has become a household name across generations—and the world. Even for a Hollywood legend like Bill Murray, Self-Interest doesn't have to mean Self Obsession.[9,10]

As kids, Bill and his brothers earned pocket change caddying at the local country club. Once their fortunes swelled in adulthood, they teamed up to launch the Murray Bros. Foundation, a community service sponsor and host of the Murray Bros. Caddyshack Charity Golf Tournament. All money raised goes to provide medical services and lifesaving equipment to the disenfranchised across America.[11]

Give, don't give back.

Whenever you give, doors open. No matter where you work, no matter where you live. The returns you see may be enough to save your business or send you to the White House. So, give. And keep on giving. Even when you don't feel like it. Even when you don't think you have anything to give. Even when you think it couldn't possibly make a difference. When you give no matter what, you attract other like-minded people who want to give, too. And as a result, you'll see new opportunities open up all around you.

Just give. Don't give back. You never stole anything in the first place. Just ask this troublemaker from Chicago.

PERSIST TOGETHER

It was January 7th, 2008. At 11:59 am, my General Manager Todd Koogler unlocked the front doors of my second Beef O'Brady's restaurant for the first time. Thanks to my typical marketing fanfare, every table was taken within an hour.

Success.

I knew it would be. I'd planned for it. In fact, I'd devoted every evening and weekend throughout 2007 and the previous three years to Due Diligence for my second location. I invested hundreds of thousands into construction and hired a full, competent staff. In my research, I found a residential developer's plans to build over five *thousand* new homes within *two* square miles of the location I'd picked out. I'd hit the jackpot! The tables tipping my servers twenties and fifties proved it.

Barely two weeks later, on January 22nd, a government agency in Washington, DC I'd never heard of rolled the dice. The Federal Open Market Committee, a Federal Reserve department worth their weight in cow patties, slashed the federal interest rate. Hours later, the stock market tanked. I guess they intended to boost the economy, but government's intentions rarely—if ever—match the outcomes. The Fed's intervention couldn't stop millions of Americans' monthly mortgage payments doubling, tripling, or worse. Residential real estate collapsed overnight. Every related industry fell with it—banking, construction, and manufacturing.[1]

I opened Beef's for lunch on the first Monday of February, and nobody showed up. Nobody. For dinner, four men showed up, but not to eat. They downed beer after beer at the bar because their employers had let them go that evening at 5:00 pm on the dot.

These poor guys were the beginning of an incoming unemployment tsunami. All over the Miami Valley, a region of a million-plus people—smart, ambitious, gainfully employed people—lost everything. Their careers, homes, and even their families. In desperation, hundreds of Beef's regulars cashed out their 401(k) retirement savings but lost their houses anyway. The line for lunch I'd counted on every weekday could be found downtown at Divorce Court.

To top off the crisis with a rotten cherry, the international residential company declared bankruptcy. Five thousand future families (and customers), gone before they existed.

In any economic downturn, much less the worst downturn since the Great Depression, people cut back. They downsize property. They clip coupons. And they eat at home. Since the 1960s, middle class America has *loved* casual dining. With both parents working outside the home, families prefer affordable meals that mom and dad don't have to spend hours prepping. With more expendable income but less time to shop and cook, why not visit your local Beef O'Brady's Family Sports Pub?

They did. Until February 2008. Estimates say twenty *thousand* restaurants in the United States closed. I know why. The economy tanked, so everybody tightened their belts. If they wanted to splurge, Beef's regulars ate off the dollar menu at McDonald's. Maybe I should've planted my restaurateur dreams beneath the Golden Arches. McDonald's was one of about two businesses in the country to *grow* during the Great Recession. Gee thanks, Ronald.

Clearly, opening a second Beef's location was a mistake. Two rents to pay, two staffs to pay, two sets of vendor bills to pay. By Valentine's Day 2008, total sales dropped seventy percent. I scaled staff back to a skeleton screw with a bare bones menu. On weekends, my team of forty-five was now a team of sixteen. And with five to seven day a week guests showing up only twice a month now, I couldn't even pay the wages of nine.

According to my plan, once my second location stood on its own two profitable feet, I was going to quit my day job. *Goodbye, plan!* I cashed out my personal savings and took cash advances on every credit card I qualified for to meet payroll and pay Beef's vendors. I took out loans in March, April, and May, but that wasn't enough.

"I've got to be honest with you," I rounded up the employees from both locations, "On Friday, I'm putting ten thousand dollars out of my own pocket to pay you guys. Next week, I'm putting another five thousand in to buy food. I've been doing this for months. I don't even know how long."

"I'll take a pay cut," my general manager and very first hire said. "If we get through this, you can make it up to me."

"If we get through this together, you bet I will. You have my word."

God bless you, Todd.

At home, I felt the same heat that burned up so many marriages all over town. With a daughter headed to college and a wife who wanted nothing to do with two failing restaurants or their owner, I was a lonely guy. Right after I turned fifty, we divorced. She walked away with her savings and retirement intact, totally debt-free. She wasn't the one who took the risk, so I firmly believed she shouldn't have to face the consequences. Alone at my kitchen table the night after she and our daughters moved out, I slumped over onto a pile of past due notices. Every thirty seconds, another debt collector called. I put my phone on silent and fell asleep in a pool of my own tears.

Nobody wants to lose everything, and I just about had. I was *not* going to lose all I had left—two failing restaurants, one job with a two-hour daily commute, and close to zero customers. Pitiful. To get some air, I called the sales rep of my apron and towel supplier.

"We're barely making it," I told her. "Honestly, we're not making it. At all. I've got to cut back on operating costs, or I'm done for."

"You're not the only one. Life's hard now, and growing a business is harder. I understand, I really do," she said. I could tell she did. "We'll get through this together. Until things turn around—and God-willing, they will—we will reduce our fee by half."

"Together." I repeated. "Thank you. If we survive, we're your customer forever."

She was right. Any business that made it through the Great Recession would face a winner-take-all market. Competition closed up shop months ago. When the Recession would end, I had no clue. Next week? Next month? Next year? I called my vendors, and most helped out. I doubled down on my first customer recruitment strategy—fundraising. In mid-2008, a local pastor along with two other friends reached out to me.

"Would you be willing to host our unemployed professionals' networking group every other Monday at Beef O'Brady's?

"Yes. Of course!"

The following Monday, nearly two hundred people packed the house at 7:00 in the morning. We called our group "The Brady Bunch." Week after week, I poured these job-seekers coffee and passed out donuts, all on me, even though it increased my debts. They showed up hopeless but left with hope. I passed around their resumes to other local business owners, and the group dwindled with each job offer given and accepted. By Christmas 2009, the Beef's-based networking group made the front page of *The Dayton Daily News*.

"If we keep giving, keep participating, keep helping out the community, the restaurant has a fighting chance," I told the reporter who interviewed me. "If we survive the devastation, we'll come out even stronger because we'll be one of the only casual dining establishments left open."

As soon as the school year kicked off, both Beef's locations saw their first profitable week in three and a half years. During an after-school marching band club fundraiser, several parents thanked me through tears.

"You helped me find a job."

"Thanks to your Beef's group, we were able to keep our marriage together."

"My kids have hope for the future now. Thank you."

So, this is what bittersweet feels like, I thought.

By next September's end, the chaos receded. My general manager received a Community Spirit Award from the Beavercreek Chamber of Commerce. The President's Club of Dayton awarded me their annual President's Award for giving to the community and saving dozens of jobs. Most importantly, I paid back my loans! I paid off all the credit card debt, and the bank restructured my loans. My newly profitable businesses caught the eye of a buyer, who offered me the restaurant-car wash swap. The rest is history. If I'd given up, I never would've had a profitable business to sell. I'd still have all that debt holding me back.

Persist together.

I juggled loans, loans to pay off other loans, and more loans to pay off *those* loans for nearly four years. I don't know if I could've persisted much longer, but one fellow restaurant entrepreneur did just that. When new highway construction kept longtime customers away from his diner, aging businessman Harland David couldn't give up.

Harlan devised a plan to partner with another entrepreneur to turn his restaurant into ten, twenty, even a hundred locations! With his briefcase, a social security check, and a midlife crisis, Harland walked into restaurants all over town. All over the state. And all over the South. He pitched his idea to a hundred business owners. All one hundred said no. He pitched his idea to *five* hundred more. All five hundred turned him down.

Seven years later, and after pitching his idea to 1,108 business owners, entrepreneur number *1,109* said yes. Harland and his first restaurant franchisee grew Kentucky Fried Chicken to over six *hundred* locations, making founder Colonel Harland David Sanders a multi-millionaire.[2]

Persist together.

Success requires sacrifice. Profit requires persistence. What I, Colonel Sanders, and every successful person have in common is fighting alongside like-minded people. If you're sitting at home staring at the cobwebs on the ceiling, no one will knock on your door, hand you an opportunity, and wish you good luck. Colonel Sanders had his first franchisee to dream bigger dreams with, and I had a staff and vendor network willing to bite the bullet with me.

If you've sent out a hundred resumes but haven't gotten a call, or if you're stuck in a dead end job, or if you can't climb that mountain of student loan debt, *stop*. Look around you. Who else is struggling? Who else is job hunting? Who else sees no future in their career? Who else can't pay down their debt?

Find these people and lock arms. Together, you have a fighting chance. As your network expands, so will the number of open doors to that next step. But if you stay isolated in your bubble of despair and don't interact with other like-minded people, you'll never make it. Why deprive yourself of opportunities? You may *try* to persist, but you won't be *together* with anyone.

So, get it together. Go find *your* together. And persist.

Together.

TRANSFORM BY LEADING

Does the word "leadership" turn you off? Does the idea of "leading" sound like a job for someone else? Is "leader" a title you don't think you've earned?

If you're nodding yes to any of those, I couldn't care less. You're a leader, period. Whether you want to be or not. A leader isn't the guy or gal at the top. It's not the person telling you what to do all day at work or school. A leader...*is you*. Because all someone needs to *be* a leader is one follower, and that's also you. Lead yourself in the direction you want to go in life, and the results you've always wanted will follow. That's how you transform chaos into meaning, confusion into purpose. Isn't that why you picked up this book, after all? You're looking for answers. Guidance. A way out. A way forward. A way to a bigger and better life. And I'm telling you, it's easier than you think. Are you making other people your leaders— bosses, professors, best friends, parents? You might as well buy a new couch if you're going to be sleeping on it all day long. And that's not what you want, is it? So, get off the couch!

Self-Leadership isn't for wusses. It's not easy to influence others, much less yourself. But when you do, the world is yours. No opportunity runs from you. And you never have to worry that you're living life according to somebody else's plan. Because it's all you, baby. Lead yourself, transform yourself. Transform yourself, transform the world. Hard to believe? Believe it anyway. I'm living proof.

I never thought about getting into politics. It's possible to make it when you have a strong base, core principles, and an unflinching stance. But I never saw myself in that world. Until just after New Year's 2017.

"What if I can affect positive change in the community as a public servant?" I tossed the idea around during breakfast with a friend in local law enforcement. "Maybe Mayor of Clayton? There's still time to get involved before the primary election. I see a lot of Veterans not getting the care they need, and it's often no fault of their own."

"Think bigger, Bill," he said. "It's not just Clayton. It's every suburb of Dayton. It's the city itself. It's the entire county!"

"Montgomery county doesn't have a Mayor." I joked.

"No, but they have Commissioners. One of their seats is up for grabs next election. Why don't you run for it? You'll have my support."

I thought he was crazy. I didn't say so.

"Let me think it over."

For the next twelve months, I did just that—and a whole lot more. The speech to my niece's class propelled me to bigger and bigger stages. I ran a social media series—"Everything Lives in Conversation"—which amassed tens of thousands of views and shares. In the heat of summer, I accepted an invitation to Chair the Montgomery County Business and Economic Coalition. The Coalition is a group of engaged business leaders committed to solving regional problems, from the opioid crisis to taxes. By mid-fall, photos of Beef's "We Stand For America" banners appeared on patriotic websites, blogs, and news shows all over the internet. Thousands of people sent me long, heartfelt emails and letters voicing their appreciation. A couple of days before Thanksgiving, the Ohio Veterans Hall of Fame inducted me into their ranks. By Christmas, I'd made my decision.

"I believe that we can really accelerate the transformation of Montgomery County into a thriving, safer and growing populace together," I said to the cameras on January 4th, 2018. "I'm announcing my candidacy for Commissioner here at the Engineer's Club for one reason: to remind you who we are. We are Charles Kettering. We are John Patterson. We are Colonel Edward Deeds. And we are Stanley Roy Copp, the individual who started the company I own and run now."

My campaign hit the ground running. Fundraiser after fundraiser, the biggest names in Ohio politics attended and voiced their support. In every speech, I spoke about serving our Veterans and protecting our neighborhoods.

About eight weeks in, something strange happened. On an otherwise uneventful Wednesday, I met with Families of Addicts, a forum of healing and hope for people whose loved ones are on the road to recovery. I shared my vision for Public Safety in Montgomery County, but more importantly, I listened. Men and women of all ages, backgrounds, and religions told me stories of lives broken and lives restored. When the meeting wrapped, two friends came up to me and said, "Bill, you forgot to tell everyone you're running for Montgomery County Commissioner!"

I hadn't thought about it. "That's okay," I told them, "It's not important. I'm just here to talk to everybody."

My own words shocked me. On the drive home, I thought...*why*? Frankly, I didn't look forward to talking about my campaign. I preferred to talk about affecting change. But all around on the campaign trail, I saw political hopefuls saying whatever loosened their listeners' wallets. They parroted my patriotic talking points in public but admitted to a win-at-any-cost strategy in private.

"Do people think I'm a fraud, too?" I whispered to myself. "Is everything I say tainted? Does the public assumed hidden agendas and ulterior motives?" I glanced across the car at the campaign postcards in the passenger seat, which featured a smiling Bill DeFries. I wasn't smiling anymore.

The previous year, I lead *myself* down a path of genuine community transformation, but I let *someone else* lead me down the campaign trail. Still, I lead the primary pack by a wide margin. If I prolonged the campaign, I had a good chance to win. But at what price? Before candidacy, whenever I spoke in a public forum or met with influencers privately, I talked about how *we* could improve the city together. Republican or Democrat, conservative or liberal, it didn't matter. We focused on similarities, not differences.

On the drive home from Families of Addicts, I wondered if those days were over. *Can a genuine man survive in a political world? Is my political journey a detour away from authentic conversations and grassroots transformation?* I thought. *Do I want to be an elected official, or do I want to make a difference?* Eight weeks into my campaign, the two looked mutually exclusive, at least for a time.

So, I led myself out of it. The next morning, I withdrew from the race. I published a campaign suspension announcement and felt other people's expectations lift off my shoulders. If only I'd done it sooner. Bigger opportunities lay ahead, and politics just got in the way at that stage of life. Anyone can criticize a self-promoting political hopeful. But nobody can criticize me for cheerleading positive change. Backing out of the Commissioner's race wasn't popular, and I disappointed a lot of supporters, friends, and family. But I am the leader of my own life, just as you're the leader of yours.

Transform by leading.

The right decision isn't always the most popular. People who think they're all that and a bag of chips look down on freethinkers who commit to leadership of self first. They're too hard to manage, too hard to control. Self-leaders don't toe the line, they go and find their own.

Just like a guy some affectionately refer to as "The Lobster." It's an unusual nickname for an unusual guy with an unusual fascination for the sea creature. Self-Leadership isn't for wusses, and The Lobster isn't one. When he warned the public about a new law's unintended consequences, mainstream media boiled his reputation. Maybe he was wrong. Maybe he *was* a "fascist." A "neo-Nazi." A member of the "alt-right."

Maybe he wasn't. No, he *knew* he wasn't. Family, friends, and students backed him up. So, The Lobster doubled down. Instead of returning to a quiet scholar's career, The Lobster took the fight to his enemies. He accepted interviews with those who'd smeared his good name. He led himself down a contrarian path, and he wasn't about to turn back. Not until he called out journalists and activists for their personal attacks, death threats, and mob justice.

The bold move worked. The Lobster's tiny following swelled into the millions. His online lectures about personal responsibility and traditional values garnered millions of views. The controversy only helped. Eight months into his book's release, Dr. Jordan B. Peterson's *Twelve Rules for Life: An Antidote to Chaos* sold two million copies. By doing what was right—speaking out against political correctness—Dr. Peterson transformed himself. And the world. Today, people of all ages, races, religions, and backgrounds fill auditoriums across the globe to hear his lectures live. And if you look closely, you'll see a few of them sporting lobster t-shirts.[1,2]

Transform by leading.

Whether you've gotten yourself into a mess or someone else threw you into it, it's not too late to lead yourself out. After all, no one else will do it for you. Your transformation starts with deciding that change is good. Reevaluate your station in life. How's that plan coming along? You *do* have a plan, right? If not, write it down! What's important to you? What is it that you want to change? What do you want to accomplish today, tomorrow, this year?

The decisions you make about the next step in your career may send you in a different direction, and you have to be okay with that. Don't procrastinate. Take some quiet time right now just for yourself. Put down this book. Put your phone on silent. Don't be your own buzzkill. Like The Lobster, lead yourself first, not other people. When you do, opportunities will line up behind you, following you to where you want to go.

I'm living proof, and you can be, too.

THE NEXT MISSION

I used to dream of flying my own airplane. *How cool would it be to soar above the clouds like an eagle, my playground as big as the sky itself?* Nope. That wasn't for me. When my family visited the Grand Canyon when I was a kid, I couldn't bring myself to the edge of the West Rim. I couldn't even *look* at the edge. Several years later back in Chicago, I took a tour of the old John Hancock Center. When everyone else snapped photos from the viewing deck hundreds of feet above the city streets, I waited in the lobby.

Then I moved to Dayton, Ohio, and learned about two brothers who built bicycles for a living—Wilbur and Orville Wright. Way back in the 1800s, they caught the entrepreneurial bug in their teens and never recovered. They opened a printing press, published several newspapers, and managed their own bicycle retail shop. In their spare time, they handmade kites and gliders to play with on a windy day.

In 1896, the brothers found inspiration for their next adventure in major headlines. Smithsonian Institution Secretary Samuel Langley successfully flew a steam-powered aircraft. Chicago inventor Octave Chanute launched human-piloted gliders. German "flying man" Otto Lilienthal died when his glider crashed nose-first into the ground with him on it. Wilbur and Orville studied all three men's achievements—and failures—and got to work in their bike shop after store hours. They repurposed bicycle parts for their *own* airplane.

Seven years into their adventure on December 17th, 1903, Orville Wright became the first person to complete a controlled, sustained flight of a powered, heavier-than-air aircraft. In fifty-nine seconds in the air, Orville didn't only conquer a fear of heights, he conquered *height itself.*[1]

When I first saw the Wright brothers' airplane at a museum in Dayton, I decided to conquer my own fear. I signed up for flying classes and I earned my pilot's license. The day I passed the test, I climbed several thousand feet into the clouds flying above Dayton.

Now, it's your turn. Face your own fear. Take flight. Reach higher than you ever have. Soar beyond everyone's expectations—especially your own. Over the last ten chapters, you've witnessed men and women like you conquer uncertainty, strike down obstacles, and create explosive success in all areas of life. *You're next.*

So, raise your hand. Yes is always more interesting than *no*. Just ask Harrison Ford, Do Won Chang, and Condoleezza Rice.

Frame failure. Mistakes aren't a burden, they're your backpack of useful tools. Remember Abraham Lincoln and Mary Kay Ash.

Do the next thing. Maybe that next thing will be your *best* thing. It sure was for Grandma Moses, Chuck Norris, and John Glenn.

Patch the biggest holes. Find your skills gaps and fill them as fast as possible. Like Michael Jordan and Mike Rowe.

Wear your badges. You'll earn the respect of people all around you, including the most important person—you. That's how Mark Cuban and Eleanor Roosevelt became household names.

Plan when others wing it. Risks can be your best friends or your worst enemies. Jeff Bezos and Sara Blakely know how to make friends. You can learn, too.

Stand up no matter what. Success without integrity is no success at all. Leo Durocher and David Asman made their choice, and it was the right one.

Give. Don't give back. Remember, you never took anything to begin with. Neither did Chance the Rapper, LeBron, D-Wade, Rudy, or Bill Murray—they *gave*.

Persist together. Give yourself a fighting chance at anything you set your mind to. Like Colonel Harland Sanders.

And transform by leading. When you transform yourself, you transform the world. That's exactly what Jordan B. Peterson did.

None of my counsel fits typical success principles. Follow average advice, and you'll get average results. But you have a much higher calling. Atypical success is a life of inspiration. You're inspired by all the possibilities that life has in store for you. You're inspired by people who've achieved small things and great things. You're inspired by your own dreams and desires.

To turn that inspiration into action, you've got to focus. You're off the beaten path in a dangerous jungle of uncertainty, the enemy's wilderness where "normal" people just don't go. So, you need a plan, and it's your job to execute one. If you don't know how to plan your raid on average, confide in family, family friends, or mentors you've always respected. Parents, grandparents, supervisors, teachers, clergy, whoever. Bounce ideas off of them. Ask them to help you weigh the pros and the cons. *Take everything they say very, very seriously.* It took me forty years to find all ten grenades. I didn't apply myself in school. I didn't take my future seriously. I didn't want extra work. I can't even imagine how much further ahead I would be today if I'd started launching those grenades much earlier in life.

Have high expectations for yourself. No matter what your best has been in the past, you can and *will* change your future and the future of everyone around you and those you encounter along the way. Decide now that you *can* change the present. Don't worry what other people think. Execute your dreams every day, and you'll reap the benefits. Like the famous French dramatist Pierre Corneille said:

> Where there is no peril in the fight, there
> is no glory in the triumph.[2]

Work hard. Fight like you mean it. You'll inspire others around you—family, friends, neighbors, co-workers, employers, and yes, your employees. Be all you can be, whether you're a Millennial hunting for your first full-time job or a seasoned Vet like me trying to find his place in a changing world.

Remember, it's never too late to be what you might have been. So, what will you be? Put down this book and go find out. Now is your time.

NOTES

Foreword

1. Levine, Philip. "from an officer's diary during the last war."

Raise Your Hand

1. Eliot, George. "George Eliot Quote." Brainy Quotes. Accessed October 1, 2018. https://www.brainyquote.com/quotes/george_eliot_161679.

2. Staff, Investopedia. "First Mover." Investopedia. August 03, 2018. Accessed October 01, 2018. https://www.investopedia.com/terms/f/firstmover.asp.

3. Pallotta, Frank. "Harrison Ford Explains How He Went From Full-Time Carpenter To Han Solo In 'Star Wars'." *Business Insider*. April 14, 2014. Accessed October 01, 2018. https://www.businessinsider.com/harrison-ford-reddit-ama-from-carpenter-to-han-solo-in-star-wars-2014-4.

4. McCluskey, Megan. "This Picture of a Young Harrison Ford May Be Too Much for You to Handle." *TIME*. December 29, 2015. Accessed October 01, 2018. http://time.com/4163261/young-harrison-ford-carpenter-picture/.

5. "Do Won Chang Success Story." Success Story. Accessed October 01, 2018. https://successstory.com/people/do-won-chang.

6. "Condoleezza Rice Biography." Encyclopedia of World Biography. Accessed October 01, 2018. https://www.notablebiographies.com/news/Ow-Sh/Rice-Condoleezza.html.

Frame Failure

1. "Abraham Lincoln's Duel." American Battlefield Trust. March 12, 2018. Accessed October 01, 2018. https://www.battlefields.org/learn/articles/abraham-lincolns-duel.

2. Konnikova, Maria. "The Lost Art of the Unsent Angry Letter." *The New York Times*. March 22, 2014. Accessed October 01, 2018. https://www.nytimes.com/2014/03/23/opinion/sunday/the-lost-art-of-the-unsent-angry-letter.html.

3. "Mary Kay Ash." Biography.com. April 28, 2017. Accessed October 01, 2018. https://www.biography.com/people/mary-kay-ash-197044.

4. Staff, Investopedia. "Compounding." Investopedia. March 23, 2018. Accessed October 01, 2018. https://www.investopedia.com/terms/c/compounding.asp.

Do the Next Thing

1. "Law of Diminishing Returns." BusinessDictionary.com. Accessed October 01, 2018. http://www.businessdictionary.com/definition/law-of-diminishing-returns.html.

2. "Grandma Moses Biography." Biography.com. June 15, 2016. Accessed October 01, 2018. https://www.biography.com/people/grandma-moses-9416251.

3. "Chuck Norris." Biography.com. April 28, 2017. Accessed October 01, 2018. https://www.biography.com/people/chuck-norris-15720761.

4. Dunbar, Brian. "Profile of John Glenn." NASA. December 05, 2016. Accessed October 01, 2018. https://www.nasa.gov/content/profile-of-john-glenn.

Patch the Biggest Holes

1. Munk, Jonathan. "Universities Can't Solve Our Skills Gap Problem, Because They Caused It." TechCrunch. May 08, 2016. Accessed October 01, 2018. https://techcrunch.com/2016/05/08/universities-cant-solve-our-skills-gap-problem-because-they-caused-it/.

2. Wisner, Matthew. "'Dirty Jobs' Star Mike Rowe: Not Everyone Should Go to College." Fox Business. February 12, 2018. Accessed October 01, 2018. https://www.foxbusiness.com/features/dirty-jobs-star-mike-rowe-not-everyone-should-go-to-college.

3. Edition, Newsweek Special. "Michael Jordan Didn't Make Varsity-At First." *Newsweek*. April 25, 2016. Accessed October 01, 2018. https://www.newsweek.com/missing-cut-382954.

4. Golgowski, Nina. "Mike Rowe Tells Grads Not To Follow Their Passion." *The Huffington Post*. June 09, 2016. Accessed October 01, 2018. https://www.huffingtonpost.com/entry/mike-rowe-gives-grad-advice_us_57597c03e4b0e39a28acb092.

5. Bunkley, Nick. "Joseph Juran, 103, Pioneer in Quality Control, Dies." *The New York Times*. March 03, 2008. Accessed October 01, 2018. https://www.nytimes.com/2008/03/03/business/03juran.html.

Wear Your Badges

1. Page, Vanessa. "How Did Mark Cuban Get Rich?" Investopedia. January 17, 2018. Accessed October 01, 2018. https://www.investopedia.com/articles/personal-finance/061515/how-did-mark-cuban-get-rich.asp.

2. "First Lady Biography: Eleanor Roosevelt." National First Ladies' Library. Accessed October 01, 2018. http://www.firstladies.org/biographies/firstladies.aspx?biography=33.

Plan When Others Wing It

1. Brennan, Neil. "Why Do Ducks Walk In A Line?" LBC. January 17, 2017. Accessed October 01, 2018. https://www.lbc.co.uk/radio/special-shows/the-mystery-hour/why-do-ducks-walk-in-a-line.

2. "Due Diligence." BusinessDictionary.com. Accessed October 01, 2018. http://www.businessdictionary.com/definition/due-diligence.html.

3. "Amazon Startup Story." Fundable. Accessed October 01, 2018. https://www.fundable.com/learn/startup-stories/amazon.

4. Matthews, Melissa. "5 Things Spanx Founder Sara Blakely Mastered Before Quitting Her Day Job." Inc.com. January 05, 2017. Accessed October 01, 2018. https://www.inc.com/melissa-matthews/5-things-sara-blakely-mastered-before-launching-spanx.html.

Stand Up No Matter What

1. Babwin, Don. "1918 World Series Started the U.S. Love Affair with National Anthem." *The Chicago Tribune*. July 04, 2017. Accessed October 01, 2018. http://www.chicagotribune.com/sports/baseball/ct-wrigley-field-national-anthem-20170703-story.html.

2. "Legal and Ethical Principles Chapter 1." Quizlet. Accessed October 01, 2018. https://quizlet.com/138925495/legal-and-ethical-principles-chapter-1-flash-cards/.

3. Littlefield, Bill. "Robinson And Durocher's Complicated — And Changing — Relationship." WBUR. April 14, 2017. Accessed October 10, 2018. http://www.wbur.org/onlyagame/2017/04/14/jackie-robinson-leo-durocher.

4. Waller, Michael J. "Will Sandinistas Face Justice?" *Insight on the News*, July 26, 1999.

5. Hoffman, Damien. "A True American Success Story – with David Asman at Fox Business Network." The Cheat Sheet. September 12, 2018. Accessed October 5, 2018. https://www.cheatsheet.com/money-career/a-true-american-success-story-with-david-asman-at-fox-business-network.html/.

6. "David Asman Bio: Age, Net Worth, Wife, Family And Parents." Hollywood Mask. September 2, 2018. Accessed October 5, 2018. https://hollywoodmask.com/entertainment/david-asman-bio-age-wife-family-parents-net-worth.html.

Give, Don't Give Back

1. Staff, Investopedia. "Self-Interest." Investopedia. June 26, 2018. Accessed October 01, 2018. https://www.investopedia.com/terms/s/self-interest.asp.

2. Written By D.L. Chandler. Posted May 27. "Chicago's Chance The Rapper Helps Stop Gun Violence In City For 42 Hours." News One. May 27, 2014. Accessed October 01, 2018. https://newsone.com/3011373/chicagos-chance-the-rapper-chicago-violence/.

3. "Chance the Rapper Pledges $1 Million to Mental Health Services in Chicago." CBS News. October 5, 2018. Accessed October 15, 2018. https://www.cbsnews.com/news/chance-the-rapper-donating-1-million-boost-chicago-mental-health-services-socialworks-2018-10-05/.

4. Johnson, K.C. "Dwyane Wade's Foundation Is Making Its Impact Felt Locally." *The Chicago Tribune*. December 18, 2016. Accessed October 01, 2018. http://www.chicagotribune.com/sports/basketball/bulls/ct-dwyane-wade-foundation-work-bulls-spt-1218-20161217-story.html.

5. Perano, Ursula, and Nadeem Muaddi. "Lebron James Opens Elementary School, Guarantees College Tuition to Graduates." CNN. August 04, 2018. Accessed October 01, 2018. https://www.cnn.com/2018/08/04/us/lebron-james-opens-school-trnd/index.html.

6. "Biography." Rudy International. Accessed October 01, 2018. https://www.rudyinternational.com/true-story/biography.

7. "Rudy (1993)." IMDb. Accessed October 01, 2018. https://www.imdb.com/title/tt0108002/.

8. "The Rudy Awards." Internet Archive Wayback Machine. Accessed October 01, 2018. https://web.archive.org/web/20090305112708/http://www.rudyawards.com/award_recogition.htm.

9. "Bill Murray." The Second City. Accessed October 01, 2018. https://www.secondcity.com/people/other/bill-murray/

10. "HISTORY." Murray Bros. Caddyshack Charity Golf Tournament. Accessed October 01, 2018. http://murraybrosgolf.com/.

11. "Murray Bros. Foundation." /www.Charitybuzz.com. Accessed October 01, 2018. https://www.charitybuzz.com/support/murraybrosgolf

Persist Together

1. Allen, Katie, and Graeme Wearden. "Federal Reserve Slashes US Rates on Day When 'chaos Reigned Supreme'." *The Guardian.* January 22, 2008. Accessed October 01, 2018. https://www.theguardian.com/business/2008/jan/22/useconomy.marketturmoil1.

2. "Six Celebrity Career Comebacks." Reed. November 25, 2015. Accessed October 01, 2018. https://www.reed.co.uk/career-advice/six-celebrity-career-comebacks/.

Transform By Leading

1. "About Dr. Jordan B Peterson - Clinical Psychologist, Professor, Author." Jordan Peterson. Accessed October 01, 2018. https://jordanbpeterson.com/about/.

2. Editors, TheFamousPeople.com. "Jordan Peterson Biography." The Famous People. April 30, 2018. Accessed October 01, 2018. https://www.thefamouspeople.com/profiles/jordan-peterson-40654.php.

The Next Mission

1. Crouch, Tom D. "Wright Brothers." Encyclopædia Britannica. September 27, 2018. Accessed October 01, 2018. https://www.britannica.com/biography/Wright-brothers.

2. "Pierre Corneille Quotes." Brainy Quote. Accessed October 01, 2018. https://www.brainyquote.com/quotes/pierre_corneille_383848.

49117229R00076

Made in the USA
Columbia, SC
19 January 2019